manifesting in

form

Eileen Patricia O'Hea
1936-2005

manifesting in

form

EILEEN O'HEA CSJ

last writings and poems
1994-2005

Medio
Media

Published 2011 in Singapore by
Medio Media
www.mediomedia.com   mmi@wccm.org

© The World Community for Christian Meditation 2011

ISBN 978-981-08-8891-6

Cover photograph: Laurence Freeman OSB

Medio Media is the publishing arm of

The World Community for Christian Meditation
International Centre
St Mark's, Myddelton Square
London EC1R 1XX, UK

www.wccm.org

Set in Swis721 Lt BT (body text), KozGoPro-Light &
KozGoPro-Extra Light ((headings)

Printed in Singapore by Stamford Press Pte Ltd

friendship

is the experience
of Divine Love
manifesting in
and between
form.

Eileen Patricia O'Hea
1 August 1936 – 2 February 2005

FOREWORD

This collection of Eileen's poems and last writings was a labour of love for her friends and community. As I re-read them I am struck by how her own labour in the vineyard has left lasting fruits and a great vintage. As she takes her place in an even wider circle of friends and a deeper community, her words will resonate in more lives and bring to her new readers what she was so gifted in sharing – detachment in love together with empathy and wisdom.

Laurence Freeman OSB
Director, The World Community for Christian Meditation

৵

CONTENTS

౨

INTRODUCTION

Anyone who knew Eileen O'Hea knew her to be a woman with an insatiable thirst for the Divine. It shaped her teaching and spiritual direction work, her writings, the depth of her interactions with the people she knew and loved, her concern for the world's suffering, her unrelenting search for new understandings and ways of expressing the reality of Love and Oneness. *Manifesting in Form* is about that thirst and the communion Eileen came to know in her fidelity to her spiritual journey.

Eileen was diagnosed with inoperable cancer on April 8 of 2004. It was Holy Thursday. She entered into her death and resurrection process, her own paschal mystery, with the faith, courage and directness that characterized her life. She wanted to live, but when her chemotherapy compromised the quality of her life and ceased to be effective, she chose to begin hospice care. In peace and simplicity, Eileen died on 2 February 2005, fittingly on a feast of light.

In the weeks before her death, Eileen wrote the essays found in the first part of this book. They begin with her account of her mystical experience at the age of thirty-four, which she describes as "the experience of knowing that God is and that I am and that I am held in love". That realization became the ground on which she stood through-out the varied experiences of her spiritual journey.

Eileen's writings give a glimpse into the things that occupied her mind and heart during her dying process. They record her understanding of meditation, conscious-ness, evil, sacraments, friendship. They return again and again to her deeply held "knowing" that we are one with and in Divine Love. That teaching, above all, is her legacy to us.

Selections from Eileen's poetry from 1994-2004 comprise the book's second part. Eileen described her poems as "the soul's song finding voice". In them, image and verse reveal the varied tones of that song and the authenticity of her personal and spiritual journey.

Like all spiritual seekers, Eileen experienced her dark nights of fear and futility and her times of resistance. Her poem "Brooklyn Mysticism" captures the frustration of such times. In it, she scolds an absent God and relegates the Divine to the corner of her heart yet ultimately awaits the breakthrough of grace.

Eileen also experienced times of consolation when she knew the joy of communion. In the poem "Tomatoes," this knowing comes in the ordinary act of picking a freshly ripened tomato.

Poems such as "Vacation" in which she calls herself "a moving sweat lodge" and "Eileen's Poetry" in which she describes herself as "an unpolished but happy vehicle" indicate her humour and humility. In "Therapist" and "The Sun Rose" the Eileen of loving compassion speaks the truth of the human person and finds, amidst the violence of 11 September 2001, "Infinite Mystery manifesting in human goodness". Other poems reveal the Eileen of varied and simple loves: the red-winged blackbird, pure white snow, the kind act, long walks, sipping tea with a friend.

In light of Eileen's death, her final poems composed in 2004 carry a special poignancy. "Transpersonal Self", written in January, three months before her diagnosis, speaks of an unfolding and ends with the plea "Let this 'I' – the one from the beginning – come!" In her November poem, "Passageway", she writes of energy moving away and her uninvited self watching and waiting. Her final poem, "Ocean Mates", recalls childhood summers at the beach. Here, Love and the beloved frolic in playfulness and delight.

෨

Eileen's poetry reflects her strong connection with people and places. She was born to Timothy and Margaret Moran O'Hea on 1 August 1936, the youngest of three children. She grew up in a Brooklyn neighbourhood teeming with activities for her and her siblings, Margaret and Eugene. Eileen attended her parish elementary school and, upon graduating from high school, became a Sister of St Joseph of Brentwood, New York. She served in a variety of ministries including teaching, social work, counselling, and spiritual direction. She studied and practised Christian Meditation and became a teacher of this form of prayer.

Eileen moved to Minnesota in 1988 at the invitation of her friend, Kathleen Spencer SSND. She wanted to explore the connection between contemplation and social justice. Initially she and Kathleen worked with the Southeast Asian immigrant community living on the eastside of St Paul.

As Eileen's reputation as a therapist and spiritual director grew, she moved full time into these ministries, working with individuals, facilitating groups, and teaching meditation. She established a small hermitage in the apartment next to her own for retreatants and for a weekly meditation group.

Eileen learned the Minnesota pastimes of fishing and cross-country skiing and cherished vacations on the north shore of Lake Superior. St Paul, and Minneapolis became her second home.

However, Eileen never lost her New York identity. She loved the beauty of upstate New York and the excitement of the city with its theatre, ballet, and opera. She fondly reminisced about her Brooklyn childhood home and neighbourhood. She treasured her ties to family and friends, especially those in her Brentwood community. She considered it an honour when her Brentwood Sisters asked her to do presentations at community events or give community retreats.

Fittingly, when Eileen died, both a memorial liturgy in

St Paul and a funeral liturgy in Brentwood celebrated her life. Her friend and colleague, Laurence Freeman OSB, director of The World Community for Christian Meditation, presided at these liturgies and gave the homilies that appear in the book's final section. They express an honest, engaging, and loving account of Laurence's experience of Eileen as person and teacher.

ဢ

Eileen and I first met in 1990. I remember well my initial encounter with this Brooklyn Irish woman whose probing questions led to unexpected insights. Over the years our relationship changed and deepened and by 2000 we had become friends. Eileen's friendship was a joy-filled and mysterious gift which continues to unfold.

Recently a colleague introduced me to an autobiographical poem by the mystic Hildegard of Bingen entitled "When I Was Five". In it she writes, "All I ever wanted was to speak God."[1]

So, too, Eileen. She spoke God. Eileen had come to see the reality of Love. She knew that Divine Love encompassed her, that she and each of us and all of creation are Divine Love manifesting in form. There were no airs about her speech, no need for flashy rhetoric or taking herself too seriously. I loved that about her, as did many other people. Eileen spoke in absolute genuineness and longing. That is why her legacy is so simple and powerful. That is how we experience her in this book.

Susan Oeffling CSJ
Minneapolis, Minnesota

---

[1] Mary T. Malone, *Praying with the Women Mystics*, The Columbia Press, New York, 2006, pp. 93-94.

LAST WRITINGS

An Ordinary Mystical Experience

The deepest part of my faith journey began with a powerful mystical experience. It is hard even now to call it mystical, because in describing it there is no way of communicating what happened to the interior part of my being. So in the end it seems as though it was all quite ordinary. But it wasn't so at the time, and still isn't.

In one sense it was an experience that grounded me in knowing the reality and presence of Divine Life. It was everything I wanted to know. It gave meaning and purpose to my life and the intense search that I was on for years.

It happened on one of the days of an eight-day retreat. I was reading scripture and realized I couldn't keep my mind still. Because I could not concentrate I decided to get out of the retreat house for a while and do some exercise. I got the bike that was in the hallway and rode toward a nearby schoolyard. I rode on the sidewalk because there was a lot of traffic in Ardsley, NY, and I felt safer off the streets.

When I came to a light at a main intersection I dismounted the bike, ready to walk it across when the light turned green. As I looked for the light to change to green I was swept up into a pure white light. Or so it seems as I write of it. However, the whole experience might have been one or two seconds and there was no earthly, visible light at all. While in this experience – there really is nothing to report, nothing to tell. No vision, no voice, no anything.

When the light turned green I walked the bike across the intersection and began my ride in the schoolyard. It was then that I felt the beginning of fear take over, and then that I consciously began to deny the experience. Why, someone might ask, would you experience fear at such a precious, awe-inspiring time? Why? Because at age 34 I finally felt I had put my life together. I finally had enough close friends, finally felt as if I had something to contribute to our world, and I was afraid that if I surrendered to the experience I had had I would have to change. So I rode around the schoolyard. I remember saying to myself: You can pretend this never happened and just push it into the basement of the psyche. This thought was a relief and it is what I did.

When I got back to the retreat house around three o'clock I put my attention on doing some things for myself, all the while being careful not to let my mind wander. I carefully filed my nails, blow-dried my hair, put some papers in order. All this occupied me until the supper bell rang. As I moved toward the dining table, where three other retreatants were seated, I became aware of wanting to sit on a chair that had arms. I felt fluid, or like vapour. I remember we had lamb for supper and thinking "how appropriate". But I quickly turned my mind just to eating the meal and trying to stay at the table for a reasonable amount of time. I wanted everything to be ordinary. I wanted to seem ordinary because no matter how much I was trying something was taking over.

After dinner I returned to my room. I was due to see my spiritual director at 7.00 pm. I took up the yellow pad I used each night for usually a rather succinct yet comprehensive accounting of the day's events, its highs and lows, its in-sights or lack thereof, which were then ready for reporting when the director, Thelma, came in. Tonight the pad was blank. As I heard Thelma coming down the hall I wrote on the pad in big letters "I HAD A MYSTICAL EXPERIENCE". When she got to the doorway, I held it up and spoke the words. I don't know exactly why I did this since at that time I did not know what a mystical experience was and had never used the word.

As Thelma listened to my words and looked at the pad I saw her eyes shift and watched her body turn to leave as she said, 'Then there's no room for me here." And she left. I was shocked. Why would she leave me at this time? I felt overwhelmed with confusion...

I have never written about or talked in detail about this experience until now. There were good reasons for this. The spiritual writers of that time worried about the ego taking over the experience and using it to embellish its own status and specialness. I was afraid of that too, so it remained a secret. But keeping it a secret had its own fallout. It also made me special and what happened to me became a unique experience between the soul and God's special favour. This secrecy had, quite subtly, the same effect as that I feared speaking about it would have on the ego, namely the sense that God favoured me and not too many others were as highly favoured.

I no longer believe this, and that is why I am now writing about this mystical experience. I am also dying of cancer and it seems as though the story should be told. Up until this time I had had many religious experiences, moments of knowing God's presence, great moments of insight that freed me of one or other of the many strings that tethered my soul. But this was, in the fullest sense of the words, mind-blowing.

Anyone who knew me knew I was a seeker. I was seeking God. I was trying to assuage some terrible longing for the holy. And because of this I went through some hard and terrible times. Some dark nights, some times when I was holding on to faith by a sliver of a thread.

Therefore, this experience felt like it was given to me because I had finally measured up, passed the grade, or maybe was being rewarded by a God who just felt so compassionate at my efforts. Since the experience was so unusual, so different from what I had considered religious experience, I didn't expect then that most people would know an experience like mine. Mystical experiences were reserved for a special few and I got one.

All of this has changed. Today there is a plethora of books describing many mystical experiences articulated by the followers of the great world religions. In our post-modern age we are experiencing collective consciousness as never before. My own experience has a home there.

Faith is no longer an unravelling rope alongside a mountain. Faith has become a stance on the mountain which holds my feet firm as I experience all the vicissitudes of mountain life – the cold and warmth, the light of beautiful days when the heart wants to say "How can I keep from singing", the darkness that can seem never ending and overwhelming. All the experiences of the spiritual journey still come and go, still affect body, mind and spirit to some degree. But the mystical experience, the experience of knowing that God is and that I am and that I am held in love is the ground on which I stand.

൭

Knowing

Unless the grain of wheat falls into the ground and dies it remains but a single grain.

Religious or mystical experience is an experience of an individual that goes beyond the rational mind or the ego-centred self. It enters a realm of experience that can best simply be called knowing.

Most of our knowing comes about because we know things from the outside. This is scientific or objective knowing. It is non-participatory.

But there is another type of knowing which comes not from outside ourselves but from our participating in it. "You are the music while the music lasts," writes T S Eliot. When we move into a deeper reality of ourselves we participate in a deeper level of consciousness and find ourselves in love. It is an experience, not a thought or even a feeling. That is why our words fail in trying to express it objectively. We were created to know and to live from this experience of being in love.

Meditators often find the transition to this way of knowing disorientating. Images, beliefs, feeling, words about God are no longer part of their conscious world in the same way.

Over the years before this transition into participative knowing came to be they found comfort in talking to God, thinking about God, feeling God's presence. Now instead they can feel a real sense of loss and grief, a feeling that something is wrong with them spiritually because the old formulas are no longer working. The same comforts are no longer present. Those things which helped define one as a grand spiritual person seem to dissolve.

It is important to stay open to the process of the transformation of consciousness that is occurring. Gradually the presence of love in the experience of knowing becomes the experience of loving. And with this comes true faith – a leap that embraces the mystery of the Divine rather than a grasping onto the consolation of form.

This is a major step in spiritual development and requires both faith and patience. All along the spiritual path the ego has known many deaths but none as complete as participatory knowing.

Meditation is not the only way of living in love but it is a direct path to it. Every meditation period means we are open to the death of the ego. The dying is in not allowing our minds to wander from the repetition of the mantra.

Once the mind is still and ego is no longer dominating us we find what we have always longed for, what we are constantly being drawn into – the experience of Divine Love.

There are two ways of knowing:

1. Scientific knowing, an objective knowledge, in which we know things from the outside. This is non-participative knowing.

2. Participative knowing in which we know things because we participate in them.

Meditation leads us into the latter, participation-based knowing. As we move more deeply into the true self we experience different levels of consciousness and therefore know, not because someone or some book told us, but because we are participating in something. What we are drawn into through meditation is an experience. We know love because we are participating in this love. We know compassion because we are participating in divine energy which is compassion.

Frequently when speaking to groups and presenting a "new" spiritual insight such as "we are forms of the formless" or "we are Divine Love manifesting in form", people who have never had this insight intuitively recognize its truth. They nod their heads in assent to the truth.

However, it takes a long time for this newly-embraced insight to overtake the embedded thought – taught and believed for years – that we are separate from God. Undoing this old belief pattern is what occurs as we meditate each morning and evening and establish the self in the reality it was created in – love. As we become more established in this truth, we begin to "know" its truth in relation to ourselves, all people, and creation.

"You are the music while the music lasts." (T S Eliot) You are love while love lasts and as long as we stay in the true self.

ص

Energy

We are systems of energy dressed in form. All energy is divine energy manifesting in form. We can say this same thing in many ways. We are forms of the formless. We are the temporal expression of the eternal. We are the finite expression of infinite Love.

These are hard concepts for most of us to absorb. We have grown up in cultures that have identified the Divine as Some One outside us, or as some one sitting outside creation and sending down or piping down at will blessing or curses, good or bad things that happen to us.

The new consciousness that we are growing into as an evolving species is teaching us something different, something new. So new that our minds can't grasp it. But we can sense that truth intuitively.

What is this truth, this new experience, this new level of consciousness? It is the truth that all is one. Each of us, all forms manifest in our individual forms, express the One who is from the beginning.

Somehow in our evolutionary process, a repeated pattern is at work. It is both psychological and emotional, a feeling of being separated from the Divine or feeling that we are inadequate, unwhole, unfinished. It is a feeling that has somehow been transfused into us. We therefore keep searching for and grasping for things outside ourselves to give us what we feel is missing inside ourselves.

It is a great moment of liberation when we realize our own wholeness, our oneness of being with the Divine Being. Meditation is a ritual that acknowledges this oneness. It helps go beyond belief systems that hold us prisoners to inadequate experiences of the self.

People who have meditated consistently know the experience of oneness with an increasing awareness. That's why they meditate – it makes them feel more authentic.

To Not Forget

"It doesn't matter if you meditate each day."

This might seem a strange sentence for a teacher of meditation to articulate. However, it is one I believe. The reasons for my believing this are as follows.

Meditation is a contemplative act. That is, the prayer frees the mind from its ego attachment to thought. In doing this it centres us through a mantra or sacred word in the experience of wholeness or the true self or Divine Love. I use these terms as synonyms.

Secondly, meditation is not an act that earns God's love or approval or special blessing. We are already – at every minute of our existence – in the experience of unconditional, unsurpassable love. That is the essence of our being. So, to not meditate, to not surrender the ego-dominated self, to not give ourselves to the daily discipline of meditation, does not fracture or break our relationship with Divine Love. It does not diminish God's all-embracing, all-compassionate love for us. But our not meditating can keep us from remembering who we truly are and the experience of total union with the Divine that we were meant to know and realize – not just after death but here and now.

To not forget that we are held in love, that we are in the most intimate of relationships in and with Divine Love is the reason for being faithful to our meditation practice twice daily. To not forget the reality we were meant to know fills us with joy and increases our happiness to the extent that we participate in it. Meditation is the doorway into this participation. Most of us struggle to find true love, to know meaning and purpose in our lives. Our meditation is a path to the experience of this reality. In other words, to not forget matters because for some it determines their sense of well-being, their joy, and experience of union. This is both stabilizing for the meditator, and changes our world.

Creation:

pets, land, sun, moon & stars

Poets, mystics, lovers of the arts, animal lovers all put us in touch with love and beauty.

The love of a person for a pet and the pet's response to the owner is also Divine Love manifesting in form. All love moves an individual beyond the self – beyond the small, insulated ego, to someone outside the self in care and response to the being-ness of energy, being expressed in form.

To hear a beautiful aria moves an audience to a profound silence. Then once the note has been reached there is a roar of applause and prolonged clapping. Beauty has moved the collective consciousness. The little individual-bound ego self is left behind and for one bright, shining moment, an experience of oneness is known by the audience as a whole.

This experience of communion that draws an individual or group to the wonder, love, beauty, goodness outside the individual ego is an expression of our own reality in the experience of love.

We are meant to be in relationship with all creation because it is also a form of the formless, the eternal expressed in the temporal, the infinite in the finite.

Some will object that this is pantheism. Pantheism says that the tree is God. The new consciousness of reality says everything that is, is the One Being expressed in and through the being of many.

Communion

We are always in communion – meaning there is no separation between us and Divine Love. St Augustine says God is closer to us than we are to ourselves. Meister Eckhart says that between us and God there is no between.

However, we live our lives as if separation is real rather than an illusion. We do this because that is what it feels like "inside" ourselves. A pattern of thought created this feeling. This thought pattern is the result of teaching we ingested through parents, Church, culture, and society.

Most of us have grown up thinking we have to earn God's love; we have to do so many good things before we can rely on God loving us. This is a fallacy. We are already in love. Because all is one, we cannot be separated from the love that is our very being. This truth, however, is hard for most people to take in. Most of us have bought into a system of thought or belief that is false and that teaches us either that we are bad or that we are not quite good enough yet. So, we have to do more good things before we really experience God's love. And we never seem to measure up, to do enough of the right things.

The fact is we are unsurpassably loved at every moment – no matter what condition we are in, good or bad. The false belief system that we adhere to like glue gets undone through our practice of meditation. The repetition of the mantra helps us collect our scattered energy and detach from the ego mind which holds us prisoners in old thought patterns.

Meditation returns us to our initial state of creation, namely the experience of knowing oneness of being with Divine Being.

Evil

If we are the Divine manifesting in form, how do we account for the evil things people do in our world?

The fact is that evil is part of the world in which we live. But according to the teaching surrounding the experience of the "new consciousness" the experience of evil is the result of our consciousness having gotten stuck in lower levels of development where we project onto others and onto the world the self-hatred we harbour within ourselves. This a-rises from the negative misconceptions of the self or creedal systems that are stuck in a particular stage of development and so not open to growth or expansion.

Getting stuck at such levels of development can afflict individuals or nations.

Any experience that creates or reinforces an experience of separation from ourselves, our world or others helps to promote or excuse evil in the world at large. Most of the wars being fought – where we are killing other human beings, destroying property and devastating the natural world – are due to people being arrested in a lower stage of consciousness that sees others as separate or as infidel. Religious wars come from a belief that my God is the one and only true God. Killing you, destroying your land, then seems like God's will, obedience to God's word.

Meditation is a way of prayer that connects us to the true self and to the expansion of consciousness that is synonymous with the deeper self. As consciousness deepens we know ourselves better because we discover that we are Divine Love manifesting. This experience concomitantly helps us realize our oneness with everyone and with all creation.

Anyone in the conscious experience of Divine Love would not, could not project harm or evil. We project onto others whatever is our own inner experience. We project love therefore when we are one with our deeper self – which means coinciding with the mind and heart of Christ.

Friendships
and Relationships of Love

Love your neighbour
as yourself. ···

Friendship is Divine Love manifesting in and between form. We think of friendship or any relationship of love in terms of gift because we feel so undeserving of love.

It is, however, through this concrete experience of love, this love manifested to us through another human being, that we gradually awaken to the knowledge that we are loved. We realize that we don't earn love and we don't have to feel worthy of it but that it is something freely given to us. Divine Love and true human love are the same reality. In friendship Divine Love finds and expresses itself in form.

Since meditation draws us into the true self – the reality of being free from egocentricity – and situates us in the experience of love itself, we become more open to others and we now begin to extend what we are experiencing in meditation to life. We are no longer projecting our own self-hatred onto the world or others and are more open to the

31

fact of someone loving us. Since we are experiencing love we are extending love.

To receive the love of a friend, husband, wife, or any person – or even a pet – is to know the experience of Divine Love. All is one. Love of God and love of neighbour are not separate realities.

Presence

There are some who wonder: since we are all one and were from the beginning of time, why have children baptized, why participate in the Eucharist and other sacraments?

If the Divine is not only totally present but totally within us and our life-essence is divine, why have such signs? The great transition in consciousness happening today takes us to these theological questions.

It is true that we are already one with the Divine. But the ritual of baptism makes explicit what is implicit. A community of faith is a field of faith, an energy force of faith, that stands beside and around us asserting the truth and directing that energy to the soul that is waking up to reality. It is jump-starting, as it were, the faith that is already there with them and all people, the love and experience that is communion.

At the Eucharist we gather with other believers knowing the presence of the Divine in all things and knowing that the life, death and resurrection experience of Jesus was that energy force in human history that awakens and calls us back into our original state – a state of complete oneness in Divine Love.

Too often our lives are so fragmented by other values or obligations that we forget. Or we become dull in our desires or in our desperation. At the Eucharist the community, the ritual, the music, the readings of scripture and, hopefully, the homily, all put us back together again. They bring us to the realization of the interconnectedness of all being.

The Eucharist was never meant to be only an intimate moment of reaching what is already true, but a means of connecting with that truth so that it overflows into our concern and love for others and for what is happening in our world. People who attend church for a spiritual high or to have their present state of consciousness affirmed or embellished risk being ego-dominated under the mask of "spirituality".

POEMS

1994 -- 2005

Enlightenment

I did not know
I had no idea –
that in loving you
I would discover
you are loving me
yesterday, today,
tomorrow, now;
and, quite dearly.
Your touch so tender,
your glance consuming –
just there –
if I dare
to look up
and meet your gaze of love.

How pathetic my striving,
how foolish my fear
that I would disappoint you,
You whose name is Love.
You are all that is,
and your love –
sweet, gentle,
an abyss of light
cushioning my soul.   ‿ 1994

Loons

Velvet rides
the water,
its carriage
regal,
its song
welcoming, familiar,
its cry
ancient, haunting,
both sad and beautiful.
As it searches
for its mate
it fills the lake
with its anxious longing,
and
remembers me
to mine   *≈ 1994*

Sky Prayer

So much to know,
or is there?
Sometimes I want to read all the
great pieces of literature – all the writings of

mystics and theologians.
Yet, I would not trade all of this knowledge
for the experience of You – your gift to me.

Is there more to understand; or,
is there only the deepening of experience?
Experience seems to go beyond knowledge
and even wisdom.

Thank you –
my heart sings with
all your reflections here –
everywhere   ᔰ 1994

Solitude

Tasting solitude,
I thought,
would be
a pleasing,
quite palatable,
rewarding
taste of Grace.

Instead,
it tasted –
not at all,
had no connector

to the brain
that remembered
me to You;
that signalled clearly,
eloquently,
Your abiding presence.

Stepping
inside solitude,
(a gaseous reality
draped around the soul)
I found
I was nowhere.
It had no space,
no face,
nothing to define
or name
this non-synapsed
experience of Grace   ✍ 1994

Water Lilies

They sit,
each day,
all day,
just there;
attuned

to night and day,
opened
to what is   ᔫ *1994*

Mandatum in the Snow

A stranger bends low,
literally kneeling at my feet.
Not kissing them reverently
as in a Holy Thursday liturgy.

No.
Rather he scrapes ice,
ice stuck inside my ski clip
which prevents me from successfully
clipping my other ski boot
to begin my trek of
moving in the
heavy layered, but gentle snow.
We are in the great earth Church,
the forest.
The candelabras are the trees,
the vestments snow.
The feast: life, faith
friendship (those present
and those always present
because they are part of me).

This stranger and I
are only two of the participants.
There are more on the trails that I can't get to.
He kneels,
his jeans caked in snow
(as least seven inches high).
"No problem," he tells me,
"I've worn snow before."
His wife watches from
her cabin window.
It was she who saw my struggle,
she who sent him down to help.
Some ancient, holy themes are
replayed in here in this snow liturgy.

The task complete,
I move on slowly, always slowly,
and join my waiting friends
in the liturgy of earth's play and beauty   *1995*

Brooklyn Mysticism

An Enneagram 8 at Prayer

You –
yes you,
have been bad!
Bad people
deserve punishment.

I am putting you
in the corner –
the corner of my awareness,
the corner of my heart.

So,
what do you think of that?
Are you sad?
disappointed?
contrite?
Are you still thinking
you're in charge?

You claim
mutual love.
I have not felt,
recognized
or known it
for some time.
Have you forgotten?
Have you forgotten me?

You
have made me weary
with your love style,
if indeed that is
what you call this.
You are
distant,
remote,
unavailable.
I

am tired.
Tired of trying,
believing,
and being faithful.
I've searched me.
I'm fed up
with looking at
what is the matter with me;
of wondering
what I am not doing right,
or how *I* could love more.
I've had it!
This fast is too much for me.
No more
stale toast and insipid water!
I'm declaring the fast over.
Do you hear?

I want
meats and sweets,
bread and wine,
comfort.
Enough already!
I want some acknowledgement
of your care,
of your presence,
of knowing
the experience
of mutual love.

Oh yes,
be forewarned.

I don't want,
won't tolerate
or accept
parent love –
"for your own good love"
or
"the Divine therapist love".
Forget it!
That no longer works.
So, keep it!

I am here
with nowhere to go,
nothing left to do
but to relegate you
to the corner of my heart.
Life goes on,
you know.
And mine –
always and only goes
because of you.
What a mess
you leave me in.
There's nothing left.
No energy,
or desire
to keep holding
you in the centre
of my awareness.

That's it!
You've had it!

You know
where I am.
You know my heart,
my love,
my total being for you.
So,
it is your move now.
Do something.
Make yourself known.
Appear,
speak,
whisper,
hint.
Do your Habakkuk
trick.
Do anything
so our love
will be fresh
and new again.

Oh yes,
a little reminder.
Your being everywhere
and in everything
is lovely –
very "Hallmark" of you.
But,
for me,
your reflected presence
only accentuates
the Reality I miss.

Don't think
I can settle
for something less

So,
if you are asleep,
WAKE UP.
If your are testing,
NOW HEAR THIS:
I've had enough.
If this is purification,
how about a break?
(You certainly can
remember where you
left off!)
If you say this
is love –
I've known you
to be much better
at it!

So,
there you have it!
It's your move.
Do something!
Anything!
Please?

P. S. If not,
I'll wait   ⁓ 1995

Christmas '95

Source of all Energy
O infinite Possibility
Knowing beyond knowing
Sweet friend
O ending life
Isness that is All
You are my flesh,
    my life
    my love.

O mystery who forms Mystery
Christ, the universe and beyond,
take flesh again, now.
Do not conceal your presence.
(Or, unscale our eyes.)
Draw, compel, direct our energies.
Align them into you.

We are fractured,
dispersed,
off-course.
Find us.
Tether our discordant hearts,
weave them to the rhythms of
Divine impulse and desire.
COME,
knit your flesh to ours,

be visible.
Console us with your presence,
you who are the unbroken
relationship
of pure love.

O incomprehensible Mystery
Word spoken
loose the hymn
we were meant to sing,
that we may dance
in harmony
with all creation.

Source of all Energy
Holy one,
and friend so dear,
You who are:
Nameless Mystery,
Faithful Companion
break through
break through
break through again,
midwife us.
Incarnate us into our flesh.
Embrace in love
our wayward energies of greed,
violence,
destruction.

Holy Mother,
gather back

these broken winged ones
to You,
their Source.
Suckle us in love,
nurse our woundedness.
Appear!
We need you.

Come then,
Source of all that is,
draw us
into harmony,
that sweet melody
of creating Love.
I, for one,
would like to dance your Song,
but I have a broken wing.   ᧗ 1995

Ordinary Time

Hold back!
Don't come in.
You ask too much.
Suck resources,
pluck growth,
demand practice.

The cupboard
is bare –

nothing there
to give,
to practise,
to practise giving.
Go back!
Don't come!
I fear,
dread,
shun,
resist
your time.

I have plugged
the crevices,
the doors,
the windows
of my soul.

Don't
lean on,
push at,
strain
the bulwarks
of my heart.

I cringe
knowing
your demands,
your lack of mercy,
your expectations
of one
already scraped clean,

bone clean.
If you know pity,
pity me.

Don't come.
Not now,
not ever.
I cannot take
the pressure
of your presence,
withstand
your demands.
Stay,
stay,
stay away
Ordinary Time.

Eve of Trinity Sunday ᔕ *1995*

Trinity Icon

I've been
here
sitting,
sitting,
sitting.
Today,
you come

sitting,
sitting,
sitting.

Trinity Sunday ❧ *1995*

Vapour God

Not empty,
nor full.
Not dry
nor sweet.
Not tomb,
nor womb.
All is vague –
vapid.
I know womb,
its security,
feeding,
nurturing love.
I know tomb,
its stench,
its horror,
your abounding absence.
But this is your cruelest trick,
the meanest yet.
Here,

imprisoned
in your love,
I do not cry out,
scream
or wrangle to get away.
A dull sadness
dresses my soul.
I neither wait
nor long for
your presence.
(Too much passion
for a vapour God.)
No, what I do is:
keep on keeping on,
depending on a vapoured
knowing.
Are you this gaseous
presence?
Are you the quantum wave?
Am I the wave
distilled from form,
wedded in unknowing?

Neither my voice
nor my hopes rise.
Is this despair?
No demands,
shouts,
pouts
tantrums,
only unwithheld love –

a love sucked clean
of desire and fulfilment.
Your lessons
coat my everyday.
I miss you deeply,
sorely,
but know your tricks
with water –
like wine and walking.
So,
if vapour is your presence now
I shall love the mists,
the clouds,
the unseen, seen.   ⊰ 1995

About Wisdom

Do not look for her
"waiting at your gate"
as sacred scripture tells you.
Rather, you will find her
in the kitchen of
your soul.
And, when sacred scripture gives you her qualities,
leading you to believe
that what she does is gentle,
kind,

radiant,
don't take it literally.
This pure emanation of light
stings, burns, disseminates.
She has a dark side –
although it is
carefully cloaked in feminine
imagery.

I have been deluded.
Learned people have
presented her to me
as the most eloquent of
teachers.
I once believed her lessons
emerged
only in dancing light
and bubbling joy.
It is not my experience.
Instead, there is something
very dull, very deflating "in"
her presence.

I shall rewrite Her story for
you –
the true story.
Wisdom is like a wine maker;
she presses upon the plucky
grapes.
Wisdom is like a kitchen chef;
she takes a ball of dough and

presses it flat.
Presses out its moisture and
its life.
Wisdom is like a meat tenderizer;
she breaks the sinews of the
ego,
then shapes it to her own
liking.

She, my friends, is not quite as benevolent as we were led
    to believe.
And so, when you hear:
" . . . for companionship
with her has no bitterness,"
you now know it is not true.

Wisdom levels,
presses down,
makes disappear
both emotion and illusion.
She unbalances you;
puts your life askew.
To know her
is to know
you will never experience
disappointment or
disillusionment to the same
degree again,
or
perhaps any other feeling
of deprivation or lack.

And, it is Wisdom's fault!
(And yours and mine for letting her into the kitchens
of our souls!)
". . .Since Wisdom, the fashioner of all things
has taught me,"
I'll make public some of her secrets.
Wisdom abides
beneath our joy,
beneath our sorrow,
beneath all transient
experiences – good and bad.
In this way she robs us
of the comfort of pure emotion.
Because of her,
collapsing into our disappointment, sadness,
loss of hope, or pain
is hardly possible.
We are deprived of revelling
in our self-pity,
deprived of the discordant comfort
we find in personal hurt –
which either activates
our righteousness or
qualifies us
for the misplaced attention our egos crave.

Wisdom, in a word, flattens.
She deflates the ego.
I know, for
today I sit with Her.
It is a very dull place.

I am neither sad nor glad.
Wisdom claimed me today, disallowing by her presence
the antics of my ego,
an ego that could easily
revel in self-absorption
and self-pity.
I am feeling gypped!
I am feeling the absence of
ego-feeling.
I am feeling a little,
a very little, wise.

Be on your guard, my friends,
"For she reaches mightily from one end of the earth
to the other, and she orders all things well." (Wis. 8:1)
O Wisdom!
Come!
Do your thing
in the kitchen of our universe.
Press out our collective egoism.
Teach us how to order all things well
    – for all women and men
    – for our earth
    – for the universe
    – for all that is.
Come O Wisdom,
Come!
We need you now.
Come!
Come!   Please come!　　　　　ᖊ 1995

Therapist

Carefully, I mark a number
within the limited space
on the professional form marked "diagnosis".
Here, I code your disorder –
and leave a legacy,
(in case I die suddenly)
for other helpers,
but more to the point,
informing those who supposedly
insure you,
that the wounds of your psyche
are terrible enough
and reimbursement is due to you.

You are not supposed to know, or care
about this written code
(although you can)
And I,
I am supposed to, somehow,
knit together your split self.

The tools of the profession,
like the machines that dig trenches into our city streets,
aim their huge many toothed shovels
and then begin to dislodge and carry off the
volumes of dirt –
until the proper depth is reached –

until your wound,
your pain is exposed.

The codes we professionals write
identify a variety of wounds:
    309.28 – Dissociative Personality Disorder
    310.26 – Manic Depression
    342.21 – Narcissistic Personality Disorder
The list is long,
but nowhere is there mentioned
what you are being healed to –
only what you are being healed of – or from.

No code is there
naming you beloved.
No code identifies you
as God's delight.
No code points to
the love duet
that is the reality of your life.

Do not let the DSM IV have the last word,
do not let it define you.
Go to the therapist.
Use her tools
to help you dig the necessary trench
to find what is beneath your pain.
Go to her knowing that these wounds
have created a hearing loss.
And know that
all therapy is about hearing.
Hearing Reality.

Hearing your name spoken in Love.
The codes for this place of identification
can be found in another book:

> "You shall be called my delight." (Is. 62:4)

> "I have loved you as the father has loved me...
> Remain in my love" (Jn. 15:9-13)

> "Do not be afraid, for I have redeemed you; I have
> called you by your name, you are mine...
> I am your God... I regard you as precious...
> and I love you." (Is. 43:2-7) ∾ 1996

Flight into Egypt

Icon Prayer

Here,
Holy Mystery
meets,
embraces
history.
Here,
love,
creativity
make discernible
both gift and giver.
Here,
a tomb
cradles new life
as the darkness of
night

makes visible
the kiss
of moon
and eternal light.

Here,
a mother rests,
is held,
supported,
made safe.
(Here too,
the desert
in a thirsty soul
is watered,
comforted,
kissed,
embraced.)

O ancient space,
sacred centre,
place of flight and
freedom,
place of death and life!
O holy time,
nuptial night
of history and divinity,
of flesh and eternal
mystery!

O timeless Life,
release in us
this waiting moment,
this wedding with

Divinity.
Saturate
our earth,
our universe
in truth.
Cradle us
in your ever-present Love.
Liberate us
from death's fear.
Penetrate us,
pierce our darkness
with this kiss
of your
embracing light.   ✍ 1997

Hell

Out of hell.
The drop cloth lifted.
Who is lifting it?

I arise.
Life is back.
Inside is back –
interiority returned.
Outside
was always there.

Where was I?
What sleep of death

was this?
It was death.
Who draped its cover
over me?
Who turned the light switch off?

How terrible death's stench
and memory!
How cruel this hell!
I roamed its rooms,
ventured its closets
– not heroically –
always wanting out.
Looking for the Exit.

And why?
For what?
I know nothing new.   ✑ 1997

Hermit

Separated
from Spring
I bring
nothing.
No lofty thoughts
no sweet remembrances
no forget-me-nots
of a heart
fertile in love.

Here
in this
empty space
it
and I
are vacuous.

Now what?
or
is there
no what.   ⁓ 1997

Hymn to the Great Mother

Pentecost Prayer

The earth is poised –
standing on tip-toe
peering over the fence of life
vigilant –
wanting to see, to know
if now is the time,
if here
is where
You will appear.

Breath is baited,
stomachs tight,
eyes are focused,
ears alert.

Senses strain,
pain
with anticipation,
with cautious delight.

All is ready.
Desire is ripe.
Hope is peaked.
Hearts are thrown open.
Earth sways,
bodies swell,
yearning,
burning,
for your kiss.

Come,
Come.
Break through.
Pour out Yourself.
Sophia us.
Mantle us in love.
Bend over,
bend into our vacant spirits.
Subsume us.

O Holy Mother,
be Mother to us.
Feed us,
suckle us in
your milk.
Envelope us,
cuddle us.

Tell us a better story.
This one is too hard,
too long,
too painful, too much to bear.

Great Mother,
open our senses
to your touch.
Womb us.
Give eyes
your sight.
Breathe us.
Give ears
your hearing.
Lead us.
Give touch
your compassion.
Kiss us.
Slake our thirst,
bathe us.
Douse your fragrance,
your blessings
upon us.
Soak us through and through.

Holy Mother,
Jesus Sophia,
Mother us –
    (Mother me.)

Come,
come,

all is ready,
we are ready.
Don't fail us
in hints and promises.
Splash into
the ocean of our longing.
Wet nurse us.
Our feeding time is past.
Long past!
Hear our cries.
Lean over us.
Draw us into You.
One us in your love.
Holy Mother,
Mother us.
Mother me.
Come　　　　∝ 1997

Night

Out of hell,
I pick up the gear
left behind
from the time
before
I was swooped
to –
some place,

not of my choice.

Hurt, vulnerable,
I roamed
the empty halls
for so long – so long,
visiting there
those primordial feelings
and places of fear.

No thought
entered this space,
this place,
of wounds,
of knowing sin.
Nothing, nothing,
nothing.
Not you,
Not me.
Nothing.
And for what?
Or why?

I've returned,
Habakkuked,
returned to life,
where
arrogance waits
like a back-pack for its owner.
Judgments,
my coat of arms,

are strewn
before me
along with
creativity,
and life's zest.
Each
ready
to be gathered,
put on,
taken in,
claimed,
chosen.   ॐ 1997

On Enlightenment

my version

I wonder,
have for some time,
if consciousness, heightened consciousness,
is enlightenment,
and, if so,
what relationship
does it have with Wisdom?

I had thought
enlightenment was a prize –

the reward of a good life.
You know,
the fasting, self-denied life;
the beating the bejabbers
out of your ego life!

To me, it seems,
Wisdom is a sitter.
You meet her
at the centre of your soul.
Like a salmon swimming up-stream
you strive and strive,
then flop,
you are sitting in Her lap.

Here, Wisdom gathers
the energies of consciousness,
like eggs in a nest,
and sits with them,
mothering, fathering them
in Her silent presence –
a presence of light.

Soaked
in Wisdom's light,
energy moves out again
into the stream of life,
creating a presence,
like fireflies
on the blackest of nights.   ᶄ *1997*

Poet?

Something within
wants – itches –
to write a poem,
a desire
coaxed by
bread, wine, stillness,
and
mother nature
sprawling
her wares before me. . .
not selling
but undulating
my senses
drawing my spirit
and poking
the heart's fire
with its yearning
for More.

I see
feel
all of it
and want
to be poetic
but
nothing comes

pages sit blank
no sound
will capture
the heart's bellowing.

Poetry
– the gift –
    is a volcano
    pushing at resistance
    with energy and light
    exploding
    expelling
    mystery
    wonder
    beauty
    love.

    Poets
    tell
    and in their telling
    gift us
    with
    meaning
    essence
    vision.
    Sometimes
    I
    am one of them
    but
    not today.   *1997*

Secrets

All beauty re-minds –
    re-members me to You.
And,
I am homesick
in this world
full of remembrance.

They are You,
    but only part.
Am I greedy?
Full of lust?
Wanting more
    than I was created for?

Yes.
That's the truth,
    and so is this:
I long to be with You,
    in You.
I am fading
from this world;
becoming odd.
Straddling both worlds
    is too hard.

It took a long time

To move one foot
        then the other
over the line.
That line where
my I
begins to disappear
into you.
But it is over
and I am in You
trying to be
in this world too.

Is this longing you desire?
If yes? Good!
I accept with love.
But know
I need help,
Your help.
Direct intervention.
This wedding
cannot abide duality.

So,
do what needs to be done!
(Another woman
        suggested the same.)
Do it now.
Now is the time.
Secrets are
        too much to bear –
        and always unnecessary
        to true love.

Here's mine –
    show up
    or
    take me home
That's my desire,
my longing,
my secret,
that's me.   ⋋ 1997

Solstice Time

White icing drips
and hardens
over layers of
flat chocolate rock.
Then, the great mother
powder sugars her
great glacier cake
with pure white snow,
wedding caking
the earth
and me
with her deliciousness.

at Castle Haven overlooking Lake Superior.
Scrumptious.   ⋋ 1997

The Wait

This place of darkness
is eternal night.
A place rich and
vacant,
devoid of light.
Here senses ooze,
lose,
evaporate into space.
have no identity,
have no place.
Here,
nothing is tasted,
nothing is heard;
here,
nothing is felt,
nothing is smelt.
Here,
eyes, familiar with night,
no longer see,
no longer have sight.

Here,
there is only waiting.
Waiting,
waiting,
waiting.
Is this a vigil?

Then of what feast?
And who or what awaits the waiter?
And who is it that waits?   ≈ 1997

Tethered

Tethered to this Love
I cannot wander far.
Its tie binds.
And tethered,
there is no happiness
outside its scope,
since freedom is somewhat lost.
And that's all right. . .
there is no need for freedom.   ≈ 1998

Dark Joy

lost point of reference

Dark joy
is a secret place
held and cherished
at the centre of being.

It neither oozes

nor bubbles,
unlike white joy
it sits unshaken
unsullied.
It is steadfast, firm, sure,
an experience
of pure delight
unmanifest in itself.
A reality known
only to the knower
to the loved one
and the lover –
whose love is held
here,
where
years of love making have led them –
where wedding
is embedded.

Dark joy is the joy of lovers.
It does not ooze
or bubble
unlike white joy
that floods, soaks
bursts though.
White joy is discovery;
dark joy is discovered.
It is dependent on nothing.
It is.
Is always.
And always new.
Always there   ∞ 1998

Messengers

Snow pillows the earth
Silence hangs suspended
The still point of quiet sits,
a magnificent air balloon
waiting for a current.

Stunned by silence
nothing moves
in the endless moment
winds hesitate
song-birds restrain,
squirrels scurry and hide.
All bow in reverence
to mystery revealed.

Caw, caw, caw
shatters sacred stillness
sleek black crows
with finger-tipped wings
screech their message.

Caw, caw, caw
the ageless whine
of sin confessing
pierces silence,
scavengers of grace
frantically beg

cawing their Kyrie
charging the air
with dissonant beauty.

Caw, caw, caw
Kyrie eleison.
Caw, caw, caw
Christe eleison.
Caw, caw, caw
Kyrie eleison.
Caw, caw, caw. .   *∾ 1998*

Wounds

A setting
of friend
of meal
of guest.
A context
engaging
friendly
warm.

Then,
the unplanned
the uninvited
the unexpected.

Some word,
story,
look
opens the wound
covered by time
and drops me
into its abyss. .   ᴥ 1998

Pentecost Dervish

Twirling,
I circle,
hoping
that you
who are fire
will consume
     my fear,
will sear
     my heart,
will brand
     my ego,
will swirl
     me
(like a funnel cloud)
into the still point
     of light,
     of life,

of love,
of You,
where all ends
and all begins.   ∝ *1998*

Light and Darkness

Summer is too bright
too busy
too
out loud.
Winter is just right –
snow blankets noise
darkness wombs the earth
wombs me.

Winter is contemplative time
earth's energy rests,
goes underground,
gives permission for interiority
sanctions it.

I long for winter,
and if not winter,
night,
and if not night,
then quiet light –
space uncharged by anything

other than divinity –
solitude.

Here
is where
I fit,
here
I sit
in energy
returned to its source.   ↭ 1998

Hermitage

When
you come
know
you never come alone.

Imperceptibly
a huge assembly
fills
surrounds
what
seemed an
empty space.

They have come

to protect you
support you
encourage you
in Love.   ∾ 1998

Spiritual Direction

a word
again
puts me
    back together
takes a spirit
    broken
draws it
from death
to life

long ago
a word
spoken
a body broken
arose
visited
places
    of darkness
    despair
    death

85

setting loose
Spirit

today
a word
again
descends
into
the hell
of self-rejection
setting loose
its spirit
freeing it
from life's
black holes   ᴥ 1998

Morning Prayer

I thought
it was
the little icon
(newly purchased)
attracting me,
drawing me
– at dawn –
to prayer

to pleasure
to beauty.

But no.
No thing
calls
carries
lands me
in
contemplative space,
only You
Your beauty
Your grace.

Another dawn
the icon remains
all is dull
flat
ordinary
the space
(once so full)
vacant
of presence.
I miss
Your kiss
what was
our time
and remember
dawn
an icon
love.   ✙ 1998

Fracto Alabastro

This
empty vessel
would
love to be
Mary's
alabaster jar
broken
poured
into you.

fracto alabastro!　　　⊷ 1999

Vigil of Night

flickering candle
burning heart
we meet
in darkness
two old friends
kissed by
night
enveloped

in her cloak
you
me
two
one

What joy
to be so kissed
so caressed.   ❧ *1999*

Prayers

My heart
burns
as I
sense
your presence
forgiveness
love.

O compassionate One
I entrust myself
to you –
  my life
  my health
  my aging

my desire for you
my future
my contemplative space
All is now yours.   ᛋ 1999

At Prayer

I envy
her
that Mary
who
back then
took
the perfumed oil
and doused
you in it.

smart woman
she
who
let longing
be poured forth
in love.

I wish
I had

an alabaster jar!
Christ: I
wish
I had
an alabaster jar.   ⌒ *1999*

Lullaby

Darkness
is my friend.
She cloaks life
with comfort,
allows being
just to be.

She slips into
each bedroom
and rocks
with her silent presence
all her children
into sleep.

Tenderly
she sings
her silent lullaby:
  "It's all right,
   you're all right;

you are safe
  here
  in me."
Then she kisses
their eyes with sleep
as her silent song
echoes
and the sky
lights with gladness.　　🙨 1999

Millennium Plea

Step
step into
the chasm of humanity.
We are split.
We straddle
beauty and terror
light and darkness
hope and despair.
Hear
listen to
our cries
the cry of the universe
and come.
Come

and save us.
Come
and redeem us.
Come
and heal us.
Scale our eyes,
unclog our ears
fill
our hearts
with wisdom.
Do not let
darkness win out.
Come Jesus
Come.   *1999*

Rebirth

Sun
eclipses
the world.
My world
left
in darkness.

Darkness isolates
makes
lonely aliens

concretizes
spirit.
Here
one must
contend
meet demons
risk
oblivion.

(In
out
in
out
in
out
attentive
to the
flow of
energy
the I
emerges.)

Compassion
births new light
restores fluidity
to spirit,
melts
the disc
of darkness,
softens
the hardened heart.   ༀ 2000

Red

Black velvet
swings
on a tall grass
trilling the song
of passion red
hiding
beneath
its wing.　　∽ 2000

Tomatoes

". . . Through the Word all things came to be.
NOT ONE THING came to be except through the Word."
John 1

Today
I ate
the sun –
warm
luscious
plump
red.

Attracted
by her
beauty
I touched
(ever so gently)
her smooth
silky skin.

Inexplicably
in some millimetre
    of a second
resting in my hand
like a puppy
or sparrow
pulsating
with life,
the gift.

Was this
a thank you
for the water
mechanically
sprayed
on a summer's garden?
Startling
this revelation of being –
of being in Being.
Where to adore
if not here,
if not everywhere?   ∽ 2000

Fatal Day 9/11/01

Like ruins
of ancient cathedrals
steel girders
   bent and empty
   buttress from debris.

The gaping hole
of New York's skyline
shocks
stuns
traumatizes
the collective consciousness
of a nation
unaccustomed
to vulnerability.

Collapsed
by the weight of loss
we kneel
in rubble
of ash
and bone
and wedding rings
murmuring words
unfelt
until today:
forgive us
our trespasses.   √ 2001

Guardian

for Rich Ruthermill, who
wouldn't sell the house to people
who wanted to cut down the oak tree

Born in darkness
Emerging into light
The oak stands tall
Guarding nature's habitat.

She claimed this land
    long ago
Vigiled winter's beauty
    of ice and snow
Manifested spring's promise
    in summer's revelation.

Undaunted by autumns
    that sweep clean other leaves
She (as all should)
    refuses death
And I
    guardian of the land
Stand with her now
In this kin-dom
of Life and beauty.
"The tree stays."

Potato Lake   *2001*

Lilac Bush

The torch
of mother nature
springs
through earth
perfuming the air
and announcing
as she
waves triumphantly
– liberty.　　❧ 2001

Pentecost 2001

The Holy Spirit
is
the ising
of Divine Life
manifesting
in dove
dolphin
grass, tree
you
me.

Her presence
burns
permeates
destroys.

We name
her
love
ghost
spirit
counsellor
friend
Life.
She is
all that is
ising through
form and formlessness
night and day
good and evil
you and me

Nothing
extinguishes
her presence
She is unrelenting
– a deerfly
unsettling
agitating
impelling us
to run for
home.   ৶ 2001

Subiacco and the Benedicts

L & E go to Benedict's cave

autumn decorates
the mountain earth
wind and air
celebrate union
undefiled air
guides
the gulls' flight.

here,
the young Benedict
prayed
here,
my companion
Laurence
sips tea
here
a telephone call
a gift
a being with
a love
that is
wind and air
here,

gratitude,
here.
timelessness
and the blessing
of the holy ones.   ↭ 2001

The Gift

You
came
in form
kissing
my soul
and
IN this Love
I –
not You –
knew
formlessness –
and
gift
and
gift
and gift.   ↭ 2001

The Sun Rose

The sun rose
keeping her promise
The moon winked
dissolving into day
Bright yellow school buses
dotted city streets
Friends and lovers
kissed goodbyes:
It was morning
of the eleventh day.

The World Trade Center
became a crematorium
Ash, credit cards, bones, rings
rolled on New York streets.
Horror was inhaled
by people everywhere:

It was noon
of the eleventh day.

Light slipped away.
A penetrating darkness
filled a nation's soul;
Vulnerability, insecurity,
powerlessness emerged.
Doubt and faith,

vengeance and love collided:
It was evening
of the eleventh day

In this blackest of nights
heroes and heroines emerged,
Infinite mystery
manifesting in human goodness
and the capacity to love
rose from the ash heap of violence.
The sun appeared
dispelling night:
It was morning
of the twelfth day.   ～ 2001

Writing a Poem

You can't decide to write a poem
Something stirs the heart
   then you write.

You can't decide to write a poem
Someone, something
unblocks the heart

and the poem begins.

You can't decide to write a poem
But you can be ready
for when the poem

climbs out of you—

scaling past hurt, disappointment, disillusionment,
(tumours that encase the heart)

You can't decide to write a poem
But you can stand naked in the breeze.

Ash Lake ᔥ 2001

11ᵗʰ Day

dark day
another one
a day
for trust
and its companion
love.

two currents
move
as night
gives way
to day

the one that leads
to doubt
and the other
which is faith.

I choose faith
and in this choice
believe
that you—YOU
are there
are here
are one with.

faith
is fire
it lights-up
day
wraps around
doubt
and moves me
into
the next step
the next task
the next encounter
the next
the next
the next...
and
there Light
there
light.   ⁓ 2002

Adventure

we
are finding
discovering
on this
great adventure
the new creation:
love …
reinterpreted
God …
beyond form
consciousness …
climbed
fullness …
in emptiness
life …
in death.   ∽ 2002

Bridge

diamonds
of light
dance across

the waves

in their path
a chair.

I sit
creating
the bridge
of light
and light.　　∽ 2002

Busyness

open
to the present
we sink
into
what?
oblivion?
and so
we keep
busy
with endless
tasks
things to be done
the list

the one more thing
wanting to
wishing to
be finished
but terrified
of finishing.   ∽ 2002

Cat

how
could you
not love
a cat?
sacred revelation
divine manifestation
scripture text
of being
knowing form
life energy
curled
into laps?
how
could you
not love
a cat?   ∽ 2002

Cloudy Day

Dark days
scare me
or
put me
in touch
with my
own darkness.

Dark nights
are comforting –
blanket me
hide me
from out-there,
invite me
in
into
a self
that no longer
has to tangle
with expectations
responsibility
concerns.

This is
sacred space.

this space
of me
finally
free.   ᷇ 2002

Conundrum

I am concerned
about becoming
and not enough
time
to become
what I now
know.

This concern
is what keeps
me from
being
what I want
to become.

"Drop the concern
and be."   ᷇ 2002

Dandelions

I could write
a clever poem
about dandelions'
swaying in spring air
flanking
(here's the clever part)
city streets
lined by high-rises
where people
stacked
like ants or cars
live;
and how
these happy little
dandelions
(when given the chance)
bring
life and beauty
to us city dwellers.
But
my cleverness
is invaded
by machinery
marching loudly
(like tanks on a battlefield)
across the grass
ready to destroy
with their whirling blades
the enemy

– my new found friends.
Then
I wonder:
What would Oliver –
Mary – write
or Keats,
Shelley, Powers,
Hopkins,
about this seeing?
About beauty
so deliberately
and cruelly destroyed?
How
would they
end this poem?
My clever ending
would read:
ouch!
They
(I'm sure)
would crumple
their writing-paper
and weep.   ✍ 2002

Does love?

Does love
become mundane?
Or do we

forget?
Does perception
develop cataracts?
Do lies destroy?
Does holding-back distort?
If these are true
a saviour
is needed.   ᛋ 2002

Eileen's Poetry

Some
work at
making good poems.
Poems of
meter
and rhyme;
prize poems,
publishable poems.

My poems
are gut poems;
unfinished
or hara poems
finished.
They are
what is
expressed
through an

unpolished
but
happy vehicle.   ❧ 2002

Feminism's Lesson

What you
have always
wanted
longed for
is oneness.
What you fear
is
oneness.
What you
protect
yourself from
is
oneness.
What you hunger
and thirst for
is oneness.

Why then
do I protect
myself from the Reality
I so want?
The past
dictates behaviour

perception
ways of knowing.
Be a feminist.
Rewrite your story
 – your gospel –
You
are its truth
when you
are you.　　　ക 2002

Friendship

to be
to be friend
is to risk
entering into
formlessness
an experience
that can terrify...
why?
because self
as known
is lost
form
as known
disappears

the discovery
in friendship
is just this:

we are
we are one
are everlasting
being
are communion
in love
form and formlessness
eternal bliss
expressed.   ∽ 2002

Gong Rings

The ringing gong
is
divine mystery
singing
her presence
into the silence
drawing those
with open hearts
into the one-ing
of their longing   ∽ 2002

Hiking Boots

When anyone asks
 "How deep is your love?"

Say
like this:
like time away
like prayer
like play
like long walks
   on cold days
like summer swims
like manhattans
   and chips
like laughter
   and sometimes tears
like waiting for you to
appear
like travelling –
is it up or down? –
the ravine
   of personal growth
like
holding hands
as we climb
the mountain of
our longing
like outrageous joy
like sorbeth
and it's descent
into dark,
steep places
that lead into
true communion.

Say:

like this
like this
like this

No wonder we need
boots!   ∽ 2002

Housekeeper

Even today
the holiest of days –
the day of risk
and new beginning –
unholy thoughts
travel my mind
wanting to
trample trust
tarnish love
re-throne fear.

But
I am
the housekeeper
of my heart:
I shoe away
the pesky dog
am vigilant

for settling dust
plump-up the
pillows of my heart
and remember
love.   ❧ *2002*

Letter to a Soul-mate

Let's ride tandem
you and I
On this
wave of mystery
splashing against
the shore.
Better yet,
let's enter the belly
of the whale
and sail as one
in the tomb
that is birthing
our oneness.
I'll meet you
there
in Love
in mystery
in the we
of one-ing.   ❧ *2002*

Life Editor

Editing
we change this
fix that
delete
insert
re-construct
and
in our busyness
forget
we are
the words
the poem of life.   ᰍ 2002

Meditation Gong

Don't
don't ring
I'm almost
there
where
I
disappear.

Don't

sound
don't interrupt
this silence
not now
not ever.   ∾ 2002

Musings

What I knew
really knew
ecstasy
lifts free from
an open heart.

Does
the heart
close
become leathery
hard
when the mist
of bliss
lifts
rises
into emptiness
returns
to nothing
felt?

Or
is the residue
– the mist –
the heart knowing
a slower
steadier flow?

~~~~~

Lakes
are pleasant enough
streams
rest in rocks
but
waterfalls
even when
frozen
gush beneath
formatted ice.

Be wary
of a heart
captured by rock
resting too long
in stagnant pools.
Hearts
are waterfalls
made to
gush
and gush
and gush.   ∽ 2002

My Fault

I
told on
snitched on
the squirrel
living
across the way
in the eave of the house
his home.

I told
and in telling
faced him
with eviction
and me
with the loss
of black
on white
scurrying
in and out
up and down
the slanted
snow-filled roof.

He is
no longer
scurrying
here
or anyplace.
Sorry little brother.   ∿ 2002

Part-time Sannyasi

Sometimes
(today)
being a sannyasi
seems the only thing
worth doing.
Is it
temptation?
desire?
Spirit?

temptation...
the move away from
this world
its complexity
confusion
mess.

desire...
that urge
to bury myself
in You –
unburdened
by –
"to do" list
no longer
responsible for –
anything.

Spirit...

that flow
(like a great river
after a heavy rain)
carrying me
into
the abyss
of self-forgetfulness
and
you and You and You.

Meditation
is that experience
of Sannyasis
who haven't figured it out
or
having figured it out
sit
and sitting
tune the heart
to life's
rhythm
just for today.   ↫ 2002

Scary Stuff

Held together
you and I
a meeting
of being

of being one.
scary stuff
this?
no
scary stuff
not being one   ∽ 2002

Seagull

You thought
you heard
the seagull screech
bellow its ache
into silence.
But
you are fooled
it was me
sounding the longing
of a heart
intuiting being
but
not there
not there.

Seagulls
are you
are me
aware

of the rupture
of separation
of hearts
cracked open
vulnerable
and with
no place to go.   ⤳ *2002*

Seepage

Joy
oozes out
slips away
leaks
from a heart punctured
by
by what?
disillusionment
hurt
misunderstanding?

how to push joy back
how to transcend
disappointment
egocentricity
love's promises?

Don't go
don't follow

the stream
that leads to despair.
Run
run
run for your life
Find
the open chamber
of the heart
and hide there.
Breathe in laughter,
set free belief
stand in trust.
Here,
only here
is salvation.   ๑ *2002*

Soul Song

Writing a poem
is not
like any other
accomplishment –
something finished
done
checked-off.

Poems are
the soul's song

finding voice –
the purity
of beauty
the experience
of being
expressed
again
as before.   ∽ 2002

The Heart's Door

I am in charge
of the door
of my heart
half-opened
swung-back
tightly shut.
It's all mine
to do
or
not do.

I am the hinge
the door
the lock
not you
or

anyone
or thing
just me.

What I see
feel
taste
what I remember
or don't –
all manipulate
the door –
today opened
tomorrow closed.

All this
the lie
life teaches
and I believe
I am
my heart –
all else is pretence.

Shouting from
or
standing behind
its bolted lock,
speaking from
its open crack,
these are the lies
believed.
I am my heart
and from here

a place sometimes
insecure
tentative
all speech
is undivided
authentic
loving
unprotected
risking failure.

Only here
do you hear
do I hear
me.   ❦ 2002

Today

Today
is the day
I have been
waiting for –
the diet day
the all is well day
the hell with
external locus day.

Today
is the day
to risk:

the truth
known,
things
left undone
telephone rings.

Today
is the day
when fear
is left homeless
(or almost)
protection:
an idle word
and love
is all.

Today
is the day
for singing
and writing
and thanking
and
being   ∽ 2002

Trio

Trio
is a cat
or is she?

She
is a presence
reminding us
of Presence –
teasing us
with
withheld love
refusing affection.

Is she
a koan
of life's
ultimate mystery.   ✖ *2002*

Undoing

Sometimes
life
gets very small.
The frames
of a moment
are frozen in
time
and
all that is
is fear
and a self
immobilized

disseminated
by the past
in the present
experiencing
the unspoken
horror
of being seen
of being known
in this
shame-filled
place.

Choice – habit
– patterns
entrench us
here
where
what is –
is now –
is lost.
Losing the
present
we lose
everything
to fear
and create
our own misery
our terror
our self-hatred.
These
are not from
out there

but here
where
we refuse
to let life be fluid
to assert
what we know:
all things
come and go.
No need
to identify
person
being
with this
or that.
Being is
always is
love manifesting
(like it or not)
all else
passing images
like dreams.

Wake
from the dream.
Step out
of patterns
and into Love
where
you are
safe
whole
free.

Don't journal.
Play a musical
instrument
or at least a CD
and
for pity's sake
don't vacuum
punishing the self.
Find compassion
compassion for the
self –
eat chocolate
write a love poem
for a friend.   ∼ 2002

Vacation

In Vacationland USA
this skin
– Irish skin –
has become
a filling station
for mosquitoes
a Mecca
for horseflies.

A huge straw hat
– dented –

weighed down
by insect repellent
haloes my head;
heavy jeans
white sneakers
unused running socks
long-sleeved shirt
are the armour
protecting me
from the sun's
fierce, fiery
rays.

I sit
within all this
a moving sweat lodge
of discomfort
an irritated specimen
of summer fun
and relaxation.

As cicadas
plague the atmosphere
with their restlessness
the loon
between dunks
hurls her mournful cry
into the air
but . . .
I am hot
and don't care
don't care

that the sky
is smeared in pink
that trees and long grasses
meet
in green
and green
and green
that the blue heron
stands
on the felled tree trunk
or the beaver
has
for another year
outsmarted
her unwilling host.

Tomorrow
I will notice
will be aware
will care.
Today
I am stuck
preoccupied
unnoticing.
Tomorrow
the "I" will see
tomorrow
the visible world
will speak again
tomorrow
I will
connect body

with heart
with soul.

But
for today
I am the icon
that sits before
the citronella candle
(haloed in my hat)
dabbing antibiotic cream
on bites and welts
waiting –
waiting for
the breeze
the night
the Arctic flow.   ∽ *2002*

Watercolour

A word
   like a misplaced
   brush stroke
oozes
bleeds
past
the boundary
of beauty
destroying

in its wetness
– its indiscretion –
the delight
of friendship
in its act
of becoming.

No eraser
for this paper
no undoing
of the word
that smears
love's canvas.　　✖ 2002

Westminster Chime

I live alone
but the
clock sings
through night
inhabiting
darkness
with its song.

A preamble –
da-da dum
dum da-da

then the chime,
is it nine
or ten
three or five?
Do I have
one
or two
more hours of sleep?
Must I wait
another hour
for the friend's call?
Am I early?
Am I late?

I stop
whenever
it sings
and listen
attentively
to its song.
Its sound
has found
a home
in me:
the clock sings
I sing
da-da dum
dum da-da
bong
bong
bong.   ⌇ 2002

Whale Search

"As we
stand on
the whale,
we fish for
minnows."
then as night
takes over day
and mind
collapses
into heart,
we become
the song
of the universe
and
the one who
sings.   ⋖ 2002

Words

Sometimes
we hunger
for words
grab books
articles

like frenzied
animals
wanting to
ingest
something
that will
satisfy the
heart's unrest
a sedative
for longing
meaning
for appeasing
the experience
of separation
and
sometimes
we find
a few
that do
exactly this.
Relieved
we move on
again as before
left foot
right foot
left foot
right foot

But
sometimes
we don't
and the words

are like
too many clothes
on the department
store rack
too much food
at the airport
buffet
we turn away
discouraged
hungry
empty
unconnected
left foot
right foot
left foot
right foot
left foot. . .   ⌇ 2002

Café

Here
I am
at "The Fine Line Café"
trying not to
think
to sink
into the centrifugal force
(so close

so close)
ready to engulf me.

This place
has rules:
not two's or three's
just you
the I
present to itself.
All else
death –
or worse,
misery.

And so I sit
sipping latte –
tasting:
mocha
cream
sweet
mocha
cream
sweet
mocha. . .   ✑ 2003

Dike

What
got set loose
today?

Poems come
yesterday
none.

What goes on here?
digestion?
weather?
prayer?

Who
unlocks the dike
takes thumb
or block away
allowing
heart's story
to flow?   ⌁ 2003

Garage Door

The day is crisp
bright sunny
my spirit is lissom
attuned to love
at one with the universe.

Slam
a door shuts

shuts me in
separates me from day
locks me in
in darkness
doubt
meaninglessness.

Shocked
I am thrown
from the back
I rode on.
Whose was it?
Which did I create?
What is real?

The stuffing removed
emptiness pervades
the I
inaccessible
or lost.
Believe
I tell myself
this is more kitchen stuff
hold fast to faith
and
ride the moment
that will pass.   ~ 2003

Holy Communion

A simple song
this presence
this outpouring
    of being
     that meets
in the duet
  that is Love.
Here –
    the singing
    the longed for
    the sought after
meet –
    in delight
    in joy
in splendour.   *2003*

Ice Shards

Gravity forgot
    (just for a moment)
and stars
plummeted
into the outstretched lake

chiming
the hymn
of the
universe. ✒ *2003*

Minnesota Winter

I drove
my truck
onto the lake's ice
(they do that here)
not realizing
it wasn't thick
enough
not quite ready
not yet

And so
I sit.
To move
it seems
is death.
I sit
I wait
(temperatures
are dropping)
All else is peril. ✒ *2003*

Morning Prayer

Heal her
   I say
heal them
   I pray
as my intent
   for the one I love
   seems
   of its nature
   to expand.
First, faces
   appear
   – those I know
   and hold so dear –
   too many to name
   to identify
   with a single
      prayer
   but I persevere
   until the
   expanding circle
   gathers in
   starving children
   war's homeless
   madmen bombing
      neighbours
   leaders
      posturing for war.
Heal us!

Save us!
I cry –
no longer
able to keep up
with the barrage
of needs
and choose instead
to sink
beyond words
beyond finitude.
Am I
a coward?
Or,
is this the
one thing
left to do?　　∽ 2003

Mother's Day

To you
who have
nurtured me
I say:
Thank you,

To you
who found
the key
that unlocked

my heart
I say:
Thank you,

To you
whose
gentle love
invites me
beyond myself
I say:
Thank you,

To you
in whom
I find
Reality expressed
Beauty known
I say
and say again:
Thank you,
Thank you,
Thank you.   ᴥ 2003

Oh!

I
write poems
to distract me
from what

must be written. . .
what must be known
what must be risked
and that
is
everything.

Risk it all
no hedging.
Go for it.
Be
be your self.

Do I know how?
Yes.
Will it hurt?
Sometimes.
(At least it will
seem so)
What will guide me –
protect me from my ego?
Inspiration
Light
Love
Intuition.
Could this project
"of being" fail?
Not to do it
is to know utter failure.
Oh!   ⮌ 2003

Poems Are

Poems
are selfish acts
– notes to myself
about what is
and isn't.

I allow you
to read them
hoping
that convincing you
I am
convinced too.

Poems are petals
– a flower I try to build
so beauty can override
my fear.

Poems
are wings
that unstick me
from my mire
and
poems are fire
my passion
my love
put out there
as gift
to you.

Poems
are selfish acts

each one
a carrier pigeon
reminding you
I am here
reminding me
I am.   *❧ 2003*

Poems Shared

here
are some poems
here
is my heart
here
I
am.
Be gentle
(I know you will)
with the presence
hidden in the poem.   *❧ 2003*

Pure Land Faith

The practice of pure land faith
is characterized by
  absence and presence
sometimes one

sometimes the other
sometimes both.

But each experience
is null.
In this realm,
there is no experience "of"
anything
pure land faith is being
being being.
nothing more
nothing less.　　　∾ 2003

Retreat 2003

How was retreat?
people
will ask.
New insights
convictions
truth to reveal?
Ordinary
extraordinary
dull and bright,
blank and full,
long and short,
happy and sad

is the reply
of the I
lost
and found
on faith's
journey.　　*ᗌ* *2003*

Sifter

Once again
the great mother
(up and at it early)
powdered sugared earth.

Once again
I am
and am here observing
her gentle
presence
as memories,
like flakes,
float
in the kitchen
of my mind:
lovely lady
dressed in white
teach me how to pray. . .　　*ᗌ* *2003*

Summer Barbecue

Joy –
like beauty
truth
goodness
love
is so hard
to delineate.
One can only
know it
experience it –
fell its delight
bubbling in you
like percolated
coffee.

No comfort
is greater
than
a visit from
one of these sisters.
Tonight I sit
in/with
my sister joy.

Ash Lake ∽ 2003

Words

Words
can be so clever.
They
can dupe –
deceive me
into believing
that what is said
what is released
is done
is finished.

Words
can be so clever;
once penned
I walk away
distance
myself
from truth,
content
with "said."

or
Words
are revelations
setting free
Spirit's
intervention

rays of light
infiltrating soul.

Words
can be so clever
that we forget
the space
the silence
the unspoken
the unwritten
that happens between
pen or sound
and allows –
fragile letters
little sounds –
to transmit
knowledge
truth
love.   ❧ 2003

Ocean Mates

Sneaker
sock
sneaker
sock
each
tucked carefully

away –
then unbound feet
move lightly
happily
towards today's playmate.

Delight
takes over
(leaving behind:
tasks
hurts
death)
as mate
meets
mate.

The ocean
knowing joy
sprays its rejoicing
and edges
its foam
to catch
the toe
the foot
the ankle
of its beloved.

But
it is outmaneuvered
by
the mate
whose footprint
gets absorbed

in the sudsy wash
and whose practised feet
quickly escape
Love's drenching.   ∽ *2004*

Passageway

Energy
    that indiscernible something
    – the ground of being –
is leaving
moving
down a passageway.
I am not invited.
I am here
watching
waiting
waiting
waiting.   ∽ *2004*

Transpersonal Self

The unfolding
is beginning.
Something is
being birthed.

Rising from the mud
of being
the "I"
filling the body
(like a slow leak
filling a tub.)

This I
feels strong.
I feel weak.
It feels resolute
I feel collapsible.
Yet,
I am still
in front
in charge
in command.
I am
the watcher
– reflexivity
they call it –

O
let it come.
let it overcome
this weak
and fragile state,
this arrogant,
mushy me.
I've been around
too long . . .
thought this me

was it!
(So many years
in the making
and unmaking)
Glad it is not.
Too much
content
identification
with a miserable
transitory system.

Let this "I"
– the one from
the beginning
come!　　　❧ 2004

EILEEN PATRICIA O'HEA

1 August 1936 – 2 February 2005

Funeral Homilies

by LAURENCE FREEMAN OSB

MEMORIAL LITURGY

Presentation of Our Lady Chapel
Sisters of St Joseph of Carondelet
St Paul Minnesota
5 February 2005

When I last saw Eileen I asked her if she had any last writings or talks she wanted me to see or to be published. She thought for a moment as she lay on her bed and pointed me across the room to look for a mauve coloured file. I couldn't find it and I thought she had got mentally confused. Quick as a flash she read my thought and – with that lovable controlled irascibility she could get at times – she corrected me and pointed me to the right place and I found the book.

I have been reading and re-reading the papers in that file over the last few days. If I read them all aloud to you, you would not complain how long it took. They capture the distilled wisdom of a woman who has been seeking God all her life and who had come to know the God who was also seeking her within her seeking. She liked the Rumi poem "Love Dogs" in which a man who has been crying to God all night and received no answer was mocked by a cynic for his persistence. The man fell asleep and dreamed that Khidr the guide of souls asked him why he had stopped praising. "Because I never heard anything back", he replied. His soul guide told him, "This longing you express *is* the return message. The grief you cry out from draws you toward union. Listen to the whining of a dog for its master. That whining is the connection."

Eileen understood that wisdom of faithful love and true

prayer from her own experience. It is why she was able to guide so many souls and why so many of us here today have so much to thank God for in her life.

Her last writings, that have nourished and moved me these last few days of mourning, possess the clarity, precision, even terseness of a teacher skilled at her craft, who doesn't have to cover up lazy thinking with flowery thought or rhetoric. They carry that sweet pain of truth that I find in Simone Weil as well, the pain that truth cuts us with as it slices through old, fixed patterns, melts down comfortable self-deceptions and opens us to the wonderful formlessness of the real. They also have that radical, refreshing humility of a genuine teacher who is in passionate love with the truth, not her reputation.

I will do my best to share these last teachings with you and as many others as I can – but not now. I think that as we are gathered here for the last time in the presence of her physical form, I should try to explore and appreciate with you, as best I can, the person herself. That is the mystery of her wholeness and uniqueness which not even the wisest words can capture. The *person* we know and love and have been known and loved by. Not just the history, career, and the developed gifts of her life that flowed so freely and generously from her. Not just the compassionate and wise counsellor and spiritual director; the mystical poet; the prudent, astute, canny facilitator of groups and communities; the co-worker and colleague; the prophet and teacher; the friend; but the whole, real, evolving person who miraculously was all these things simultaneously, sometimes one sometimes the other according to the needs of the moment and the person she was with.

I will inevitably miss out a lot from this attempt and you can add much more to the picture of the Eileen that each of you knew and loved.

୬

I'm sure that in recent months we have all been thinking about Eileen the person as we knew her, as she progressed in her dying and as she continued to learn and teach from within that hard school of death. Haven't you thought where you first met her? When you began to realize what an unusual individual she was? How stubborn she could be in her fierce integrity? How kind she was and yet how foreign sentimentality was to her personality? How sensitive, even touchy and yet so reserved and private in her need for her own space? How she gave herself so generously and yet respected the boundaries of silence in relationships? How she liked wine and food and movies and interesting new places and yet had such a passion for expanding her knowledge, for ideas and pushing back her mental horizons? How serious she was, and also how quickly her sense of the absurd or her pleasure in seeing pomposity pricked could send her off into a burst of wild and infectious laughter. I used to love hear her laugh like that.

You see how when we start describing a person we are also describing ourselves? Especially when the person is a friend. All that in us clicks with, resonates with and resembles the friend and, equally, all that makes them different from us. No wonder human friendship is the best introduction to God. Friends are always alike and different. As Aristotle said, the friend is "another oneself". Every person is a drama of opposites and creative tensions. That is why friends must be truthful with each other. Eileen had the spirit of truth. Friends must be equal, even with a disparity of gifts. Eileen never dominated. Friends must wish each other's well-being. Eileen had no ill-will.

In its highest form, friendship is a manifestation of the divine life in human form, the friendship of the Trinity that is the ground of all being, the source and goal of creation. This is why I felt the Spirit of Christ to be so *really* present when I visited Eileen a few days before she died and saw the extraordinary loving care and devotion she was receiving in such a radiant way from her dear friend Susan and her sister Peg, from the hospice care nurse and in many other ways from her beloved CSJ sisters in Minneapolis, and Brentwood, the spiritual family she was so faithful to, so deeply identified with; and from her friends and students far and wide. As St Aelred says, when two friends reach that level together Christ forms a third between them.

Although I said I wouldn't, here let me quote Eileen in a piece from that mauve file she titled "Friendship":

> Friendship is the experience of Divine Love manifesting in and between form. We think of friendship or any relationship of love as a gift, because we feel so undeserving of love. It is, however, in this concrete experience of love – this love manifested to us through another human being – that we gradually awaken to the experience that we are loved. We don't have to earn or feel worthy of it. Divine love and true human love are the same.

Eileen learned this, above all, by being so *conscious* in all her relationships. She called human relationships the "sacred ground of our lives". And she knew, as a psychologist first of all, that the state of our relationships more than anything else – more than power, fame, money or success – determines the quality of life. Eileen learned this by being a friend, at the appropriate level, with everyone, within the boundaries that expressed the truth of the relationship. It was a great part of her wisdom and how she helped so many people live better and fuller lives through their relationships. Everyone who knew her benefitted from the encounter with her sensitive wisdom about relationships. So we can say:

> *Her very person was a manifestation of grace. It was a grace to know her.*

This grace began for me in 1981, one hot summer day in Montreal during a rainstorm. I welcomed Eileen and a friend she came with to the monastery where I then lived. She had come to find out what we were teaching about Christian meditation. We were a struggling young community and we put our guests, even the most spiritual, to manual labour. I asked her if she'd like to do some and she said yes. She didn't suspect I was going to get her washing down walls and the high ceiling in our new chapel. But she did it and it wasn't until years later, when I heard her tell the story, that I realized how surprised she had been and presumptuous I had been. But Eileen was nothing if not a person who liked an adventure and she was not put off easily from beginning one. Her adventure on that visit led her to an inner journey for which she was already well-prepared. She intuitively understood everything she learned from John Main and the contemplative tradition and that is why she was able to become such a profound and original teacher of this way. In the years since that visit, her talks, retreats, books and tapes have led many to the practice of meditation and so to a deeper union with God and their true selves.

Of all the retreats I have led with her over the years and all the projects we have shared perhaps the one that still touches the most lives is the School of The World Community for Christian Meditation. She helped me begin the School; and in those early stages she wisely and cleverly shaped its nature and direction.

Her person was innately that of a disciple and a teacher

I'm sure if she was preaching at my funeral she would have told the story of the ceiling. She pointed out many of my faults to me over the years, some of which I even agreed with. (To describe a friend shows as much about the teller as the subject.) With Eileen as a friend you came to know yourself better. So we can also say

Her person was a bolt of truth. It was a catalyst to clear awareness.

What little have I been able to say so far about the person of Eileen? That her friendship was grace and truth, more and more intensely through the years of the friendship. Like Christ who is "full of grace and truth" and came among us as the human form of the Formless One. That she learned and taught with an equal passion. That she had the effect of raising consciousness with those she was in relationship with. That she had the charism both of a teacher and a prophet.

Her Christian faith evolved along with her personal maturity, as it should have done but as it often fails to do in many religious people. It saddened and angered her when she met people or institutions that refused, for fear of change or arrogance, to evolve. With each stage of her Christian maturing she felt her way forward, led by intellect and curiosity but also by wit and intuition. When she was struck by a new idea, a new vision of reality she explored it. But she also explored *with it*, as one more precious tool that the Holy Spirit of Wisdom had given her to pursue her quest.

Her embracing of Buddhism, Zen and Tibetan, of Rumi, of the *Upanishads* and her responsiveness to all faiths, developed on that solid foundation of good Brooklyn-Irish Catholicism whose value she never lost sight of – and never lost.

I once asked her to accompany me on a visit to the Dalai Lama in his residence in the Himalayas. She accepted willingly despite her grave anxieties about physical travel in India. I was struck by her courage in overcoming these cultural fears. I promised to make things as smooth as possible. Knowing me, she kept asking if I had reserved a hotel for our first night in India. I did not get off to a good start when I confessed on the plane that I had forgotten. But, I assured her, "When we arrive, I'll go straight to the hotel desk at the airport. No problem." She looked at me quizzically and said nothing, the Eileen look. At 2.00 am when we landed in Delhi I did go to the desk while she nervously guarded the baggage, and I was pleased to find two rooms available at the Sheraton for $10.00 a night. I thought I had redeemed myself. But, as the taxi took us past the luxury hotels and then off the main street and into the seedy back alleys, I feared the worst. We pulled up outside a small flea-pit which was indeed accurately but not truthfully called "The Sheraton". She said nothing but her look again said everything. I had failed. When I called to her room next morning she was lying rigid on the bed fully dressed with overcoat and shoes still on. But she forgave me and battled on with our adventure and she loved every minute of it, or almost every minute.

At the Good Heart Seminar she had asked the Dalai Lama if he would like to meet Jesus and if so what would he like to ask him. The Dalai Lama replied astutely that, yes, he would, and he would ask "what is the nature of the Father?" "Very good," said Eileen approvingly and added, "of course many today would say 'and of the Mother' too." When we met him in Dharamsala, knowing of his mechanical love for fixing things, she gave him a tool kit she had bought and carried all the way from Minneapolis. With her we planned the next stage of the Good Heart dialogue that was to become the "Way of Peace". I was grateful then as always both for her good counsel and her positive encouragement. I was proud to have her beside me representing not only the World Community but Christianity as well. I would add then to her list of personal attributes:

Her person was Christ-centred. It was rooted in Jesus and it loved to explore the many mansions of his Father's house.

It seems so bizarre to be talking about Eileen like this, describing her, summarizing her, as if she were dead. And she is, isn't she? So, we are left with a one-sided

174

conversation with a dear friend of so many years. We might find ourselves saying, *Eileen what do you think of this? Eileen, I've got something to tell you. Eileen, what's happening with you? What are you learning and teaching these days?* And there will be no answer, no call back, no message on the answering machine, "this is Eileen, call me", no e-mail (although she was never much use at e-mail), no long chats that renewed friendship and restored enthusiasm for the pilgrimage of life.

That's death for you.

Our personal lives and the life of the Church in which she was an exemplary role model for women, have been diminished by her death. Let's be honest. No words, no platitudes, no beliefs can reverse it. He cried "Eli, eli lama sabacthani" and gave up his spirit. And darkness covered the land. And the veil of the temple was split in two.

There is no sense in Resurrection until we face the fact that the light has gone out.

Yet there are the first fruits, the first streaks of the eternal day. We are celebrating these here and now in our friendship with Eileen, a friendship in which Christ forms the third between us and in whom we find ourselves in closer union with each other *because* he is between us. I saw these fruits already in her at our last meeting. Sitting with her I knew I was in the tabernacle of Presence. When I asked her how she was feeling, she replied that "feeling" was not a relevant term any more. She *knew* she was loved. She *knew* she was in the light. She *knew* she would stay in touch and be present through the years ahead.

The day after she died I briefly felt or saw her smile – if "feeling" or "seeing" are the right metaphors. It said nothing and everything. It was full of grace and truth. It was the smile of the beatific vision, peaceful, loving, all-compassionate, all-healing and all-forgiving, all-understanding. The smile of a person who knows without the shadow of self-consciousness that she is loved and so who now *is* purely

175

loving. The person who has come to be fully herself, all the tensions, contradictions and struggles resolved, all desires transformed and fulfilled. Augustine said that the beatific vision is not everyone in an audience looking up at God on the divine stage but each person looking directly into each other's eyes and seeing God *in* the other. Eileen is still Eileen. But she is wholly the person God knew from the beginning of time and has so carefully led into being the person She was calling her to be. We can say then,

> *Her person is in God. It is divine. Between her and God there is no between.*

This will not be altogether a surprise for her. All her life she has been preparing for it. The "outrageous hunger" she often spoke about and felt so intensely has been sated. What we are doing here is a small sideshow to the performance she is part of. And yet because of the divine nature of friendship, the depth and purity of the person she was, the person she *is,* not the person she was, is with us here, celebrating with us, seeing God in us, God-in-her.

Her decisive mystical experience at the age of thirty-four was a sudden, unexpected surge of consciousness that made the whole process of her life thrill to the adventure and grace of human existence. She wrote so honestly and clearly about this experience in her last writings that she had clearly grown into a rare and free detachment from it. She described how she had wanted to pretend afterwards that it hadn't happened but also that, when she did acknowledge it, she couldn't describe it adequately and so "in the end it seems as though it was all quite ordinary". She was on retreat and feeling distracted so went for a bike ride. She dismounted at a signal on a main intersection.

As I looked for the light to change to green I was swept up into a pure white light – or so it seems as I write of it. The whole experience might have been one or two seconds.. There is really nothing to report, nothing to tell. No vision, no voice, no anything. When the light turned green I walked the bike across the intersection and began my ride in the school yard. It was then I felt the beginning of fear and then that I consciously began to deny the experience.

Later, in her room, she asked herself why she felt this desire of denial and she knew it was because of the fear of changing. That day she overcame the fear that keeps so many of us from being fully the person we are called to be, free, loving and joyful. Eileen had her dark nights after this experience of the green light (trust someone called O'Hea to make it a green light). But she never lost touch with that pure white light which she knew to be love and knew to be in her deepest being and in every being. She knew this beyond words and thoughts and she could reveal it to people as a truth of their own being.

This experience became as it was no doubt meant to be in God's loving design for her person, a foundation for the rest of her life. There were ups and downs. As she said,

All the experiences of the spiritual journey still come and go, still effect body, mind and spirit to some degree. But the mystical experience, the experience of knowing that God is, that I am and that I am held in love is the ground on which I stand.

This is why she was not just another person but a special person. And why she wanted us all to know there is nothing special about being special. So (she knew) are we all. The process of change that caught her up in itself was the divine energy. It became so conscious and evident in her and yet it was nothing but the universal process of human development, what the early Christian teachers called *theosis*, divinization. If we have lost her to that, why should we complain? God became human so that all human beings could become divine. In recent years Eileen liked to express this Christic mystery in terms of energy and I will end with some of her words about energy:

> We are systems of energy dressed in form. All energy is divine energy, manifesting in form. We can say this same thing in many ways: we are forms of the formless; we are the temporal expressions of the eternal; we are the finite expressions of infinite love.

It is enough to say now about the person of Eileen, our beloved sister, friend, teacher and companion that

> *Her person is an expression of infinite love. She is one with the energy of love.*

Let us praise God for that, for her and *with* her.

MASS OF CHRISTIAN BURIAL

Sacred Heart Chapel

Sisters of St Joseph of Brentwood
Brentwood, New York
9 February 2005

When I arrived here last night the first thing I did after being shown my room was join the meditation group that meets here at the Mother House every week. It was a moving sign to me of Eileen's enduring presence and her deep influence on this community that she loved so dearly and that loved her so faithfully. That is one very important thing we are celebrating in this mass.

It is a sign of Eileen's unusual personality and the richness of her life in community that she is having two funeral masses: last Saturday in Minneapolis where she lived for the past 20 years; and today, Ash Wednesday, when we are all reminded of our mortality and frailty, here in Brentwood where she began her religious life 51 years ago, here where her roots remained fresh and lovingly tended. It is a gift for me to share our loss and grief together, and also our faith; to mourn but also to celebrate with you, her own Sisters of St Joseph, the life and work of a dear friend and my close colleague in The World Community for Christian Meditation of which she was a founding and Guiding Board member.

In Minneapolis a few days ago I reflected on Eileen's personality, a complex, subtle, clear, truth-filled, idiosyncratic, loving personality marked especially with the charism of prophet and friend. Tonight I would like to try to explore another of her charisms and the one that perhaps has had the most far-reaching influence, her great gift as a teacher.

❧

She was a pilgrim in the spiritual realms and a theologian. Not a theologian in the academic sense but in the sense of the Christian Desert tradition which said that "the theologian is one who prays and one who prays is a theologian". She was an explorer of these pathways of the spirit, always seeking the next connection, the next transition in understanding. This questing, questioning, curious, challenging approach to life and her own ways of making meaning of life seem to have been part of her character even as a child. She always had a strong trust in her own sense of truth and justice. She could learn from others but she was quick to assess and if necessary contest their authority. This probably strengthened her solitary character – not an isolated or even lonely character – but a character that had early on found and embraced its own uniqueness.

Her ideas about God, the Church, the role of women, religious life and the spiritual journey, all developed over time. They ought to have changed, of course, in a woman whose experience spanned nearly 70 years, who entered religious life in 1954 and died, faithful to her original vows, in 2005. Her excellence as a teacher derived from the diversity of her religious and theological conditioning and her professional training in other fields, from primary school teaching, to social work, family therapy and, in her maturity, from her spiritual direction, retreats and the way she taught the contemplative life as a teacher of Christian meditation. It is no small tribute to her religious family here in Brentwood that you were able for half a century to provide such an unusual individual with a continuum of community and affirmation in which she could evolve and mature in all these fields and find, by the end of her life, such a remarkable, distinctive integration.

I can't do justice to her journey and to her gifts as a teacher. Many of you, and all of you as a community, will want to complete what I attempt. Many of you have bene-fitted personally from her sharing with you of her explorations and discoveries. As a teacher she had a freshness, a depth and an excitement – a strong but joyful seriousness – that she communicated both in the spoken word (the primary medium of all teaching) as well as in her articles, books, poems and tapes. She laboured long and hard over all her talks and retreats. Writing was a labour for her although one that she enjoyed. When she took her sabbatical to write in a trailer in West Virginia she followed the discipline of the writer as well as the hermit. She once described to me the writer's pleasure in finding the work in progress waiting for her on her desk each morning. In all these varied media she learned to teach what she had acquired in the cell of her self-knowledge.

I would like to take two areas of her teaching and try to see where she had reached in each of them by the end of her life: before she entered into that full personal union with Truth itself that she longed and thirsted for all her life. From that union in which she is complete and silent now I am sure she will continue to teach us through the Holy Spirit of Truth that Jesus breathes into us.

Firstly, she was gripped passionately by the essential religious question, the meaning of God and the nature of our experience of God. Her journey in this field of enquiry, of basic theology, shows her as a child of her time. It began in the old dramatic, dualism of God. Pre-Conciliar Catholicism sharply drew a picture of God as outside and above us, a God with whom we communicated primarily through the intermediaries of sacraments and clergy - or the occasional exceptional religious. She arrived by the end of her life at a very different sense of God shaped by a perception and by her own experience of mystical union. This different sense of who God is had been formed by several influences, her own inner journey, her grasp and understanding of the divine feminine, her research into the Christian contemplative tradition and her dialogue with other religions. She began like most of us with a dominant mental image of God, patriarchal, judgemental, frightening, yet, for all that, not all bad. It was also awesome, transcendent and loving. I guess that her rebellious personality – that many of you knew well and which was manifested very early when she defiantly dated the Italian boys that her father declared unsuitable for a good Irish girl, or indeed any Irish girl – derived from these contradictory images of God in conflict within her. The dualistic God, the split personality of the Divine could never have made sense to her. She rejected it while of course being influenced by it. The true, living image of God was so deeply and consciously alive in her deep self, however, that it meant everything to her to get it right, to understand and relate to it clearly and truthfully. This was a struggle for her.

She achieved it, not in the realm of abstract theology or God-talk but of human psychology. The connection between the image of God and the relationship of a person with herself was central to her wisdom as a teacher. She and I had many conversations over 24 years of friendship about the role of therapy in the spiritual journey. We explored and argued about the relation between psychology, theology and meditation. They were conversations which often challenged me and taught me much.

She believed, empirically, that you had to get down into the deep operating system of the person, into the very nature of Mind and consciousness, before the right idea – the right ikon – of God could be realized. This turned the old pre-conciliar idea of sin on its head. Once you take the actual and whole human person as the starting-point to God, sin could no longer be seen in the old dualistic model. It is not just a simple, wilful disobedience of Divine or Ecclesiastical commandments, a breaking of rules for which we will be punished or reprieved. Goodness too, therefore, is not a conformist law-abidingness which the Father will reward. The legalization of sin which Christianity exposes as the great religious illusion and supposedly replaces with the law of grace was a clear personal discovery for Eileen through her work as a therapist. It set her free for the deeper explorations of God she made.

ॐ

She saw, in herself and in those she worked with, that the nature of sin is illusion and that it is the cause of suffering and psychological dysfunction. It is also the root of our inability to love.

> Our wounds, those unhealed parts of the self – the afflicted ego – keep us from truly realizing what is always there. Love, pure love. If we knew at the deepest level the experience of this love, our wounds – that is, our self-doubt, confusion, guilt, fears, our being not enough – would all be absorbed in love and we would know freedom, peace joy. Most of us are not there yet. But we are on the way.

> We live our lives (she wrote towards the end of her life) as if separation is real rather than an illusion. She wondered why we all fall under the sway of this illusion and concluded that it is simply because that is what we feel we are like in ourselves. What creates this all-powerful feeling? In her later teaching she identified it as a thought pattern that resulted from bad teaching – the mis-information about our very selves, the de-formation that we suffer at the hands of parents, Church, culture and society.

> In religious terms this pattern of thought leads us to believe that we have to earn God's love by doing good things and by avoiding bad things. Good and Bad are culturally relative ideas but we ingest them as absolute standards identified with particular ways of behaving along with absolute sanctions, rewards and punishments. It is

hard, she said, for most people so culturally conditioned and religiously trained to take in the real truth of the Gospel: that there is no separation between us and God; and that we don't have to earn God's love, because it is our very being.

The fact is that we are loved unsurpassably at every moment no matter what condition we are in, good or bad.

In this we can hear the echo of the true Christian tradition, the voice for example of Mother Julian of Norwich for whom sin has only the reality and influence of an illusion and which is utterly evaporated upon contact with the love of God.

The false belief system denies this fact. It constructs an essentially fantasy world of punishment, reward, self-deception and pious role-playing as well, more ominously, an often repressed, self-tormenting hatred of the very God who loves us and whom we are created to love. This premise became more and more essential to her teaching throughout her life. The great Christian mystics reassured her that she was on the right track. She loved Meister Eckhart for this reason, who said that "between me and God there is no between". But so also did Rumi and the Hindu scriptures and the teachings of the Buddha.

Because she was rooted in these great spiritual and philosophical traditions she did not succumb to a facile optimism or a New Age denial of evil. She encountered it in her work and saw it at work in the world. People do terrible things, to themselves, to those they love, to their enemies and also to innocent defenceless strangers. She recognized that evil is part of the world we inhabit. The old dualism explained it away conveniently just as "the work of the devil". Her contemplative, psychological perspective confronted it more honestly. Evil, she said, is the projection of our own self-hatred, the negative and false conceptions of self. It is also the attempt to impose on others the creedal belief systems formed in this negative and arrested stage of human development. This was her way of understanding evil in both personal and social terms.

Feeling separate ourselves, we see others as separate: the environment, immigrants, other races or faiths, the poor. What we see as separate we feel alright about rejecting and destroying. Any belief, she thought, whether religious or political or personal, that reinforces the experience of separation from ourselves or others, helps to promote if not to actually cause evil in our world.

This was her final diagnosis of the human problem of suffering and evil, sin, shame, guilt alienation and violence. In her discovery of meditation in the Christian tradition she understood and went on to teach the response to it. She saw that the cure is not an ideology but a practice. Even when she understood the compulsive, pathological root of sin and evil, she saw we are not totally relieved of all responsibility. We are responsible in part for our own cure. In collaboration with the Spirit we are our own therapists. Meditation is a discipline, a responsible response to the fact of our own woundedness. In John Main, whose tapes she often used to listen to at breakfast, she recognized an authority she could trust. Through his teaching she found a connection to the greater contemplative tradition which nourished her ever after.

Eileen understood that the false belief system that creates a false God is resilient to ideas. The cure is the way of self-knowledge, and self-knowledge cannot be given. It is an experience to be broken into, through the cooperation of faith and grace. But you "gotta do the work yourself". The illusions that "we adhere to like glue" get undone through the practice of meditation.

The repetition of the mantra helps us collect our scattered energy and detach from the ego mind which holds us prisoner in our old thought patterns.

A Zen saying that she chewed on for many years invites us to find the "original face we had before our parents were born". For her, this meant the way meditation restores us to our initial state of creation – she remained within the Biblical myth – which is the experience of "knowing oneness of being with divine being".

For Eileen, therefore, meditation has meaning and is effective at the spiritual, psychological and social levels. It is the essential therapy, the healing of the painful, core sense of separation and shame. It restores us from the fallen human condition. Her insight into the fundamental importance of contemplation for all human situations and personalities; is very like that of *The Cloud of Unknowing*. For *The Cloud,* too, this "work of contemplation dries up the root of sin within you". Psychotherapy is an important preparation for the therapy of the prayer of the heart. And contemplation is the necessary therapy for the deformities of religion that false belief systems create.

Eileen was a uniquely individual teacher of this tradition. She could not buy anything as a package that she did not make her own; but I knew that when she taught meditation we were operating on the same wavelength. She introduced her clients and directees to meditation when she felt they were ready, and she had an intuitive gift for sensing the right moment. In her teaching within the World Community, especially on the retreats that we led together, and many of you who followed her retreats here will recognize this, she was a strict enforcer of the silence and mindfulness which is the ideal context for the practice.

Meditation is a way of prayer that connects us to our true self and the expansion of consciousness that is synonymous with the deeper self.

The Christian contemplative tradition has always taught and she too saw that meditation is a way of self-knowledge: it helps us experientially to realize that "we are Divine Love manifesting". Hence, her insight into the nature of the Self as expanding consciousness, not a thing we find "inside us", a fixed point of ego-objectification. No one in whom this conscious experience of union was awakening could do harm or promote evil. We project onto others our own inner experience. Or, as Jesus said, it is what comes out of the heart of a person that matters. So, when we are one with our deepest self we project or emanate love. And, she insisted, this is the experience that coincides with the mind and heart of Christ. "Since we experience love we extend love," she said succinctly.

She took meditation seriously because she knew it was the real thing. She did not say, any more than John Main did, that meditation is the only way into the experience of what she called "living in love" but, she did say "it is a direct path to it".

Meditation is a way of opening ourselves to the experience of the Holy – of going beyond our finite concepts and realizing, experiencing oneness with the divine. Anyone who meditates expresses a willingness to go beyond form and therefore a willingness to suffer or die to the comfort they have grown accustomed to through a belief in form.

Not easy, because it involves a transcendence of the rational mind and the ego-centred self and an entry into a new kind of knowing. By knowing, here, she means something different from our habitual externally-oriented perception. The other type of knowing she was interested in is "participative" knowing which is an experience not of thought or feeling but of love itself. It is so important, so fundamental because "we were created to know and live from this experience of being in love". It is our very meaning as human beings.

People who have been meditating for some time often find this transition from objective to participative knowledge disorienting because images, beliefs and feelings about God and themselves lose their old relevance. Previously they found comfort and solace in talking to God, thinking about God. Like St John of the Cross, Eileen knew as a contemplative teacher that she had to help people through this dark night of the senses and she knew the route well herself.

A real experience of loss and grief – a feeling that something is wrong with me spiritually because the old formulas are no longer working: the same comforts are no longer present. These things which helped to define one as a good spiritual person seem to dissolve.

That lack of sentimentality, that at times abrupt directness that were part of her way of being even with friends, especially with friends, was consistent with her relationship with God. She must have treated God the way she treated her friends! In someone who had not persevered with this journey this could have led to a bitterness or corrosive sadness. But she had discovered that

Gradually the presence of love in the experience of knowing becomes the experience of being and with it comes the experience of true faith – a leap that embraces the mystery of the divine rather than a grasping onto the consolation of prayer.

This is a major step in spiritual development. It requires faith and practice. It is the most complete of all the many deaths the ego has to undergo along the spiritual path. Yet it is worth the struggle because

Once the mind is still and ego is no longer dominating us, we find what we have always longed for – what we are constantly being drawn into – the experience of Divine Love.

This is a spiritual teacher at the height of her powers. I cannot understand why Eileen has been taken away from us and from the Church when there is so great a need for women of her depth and wisdom. She could have had longer. And yet that is not for us to say. We can see that her work as a teacher made a profound, transformative impact on many, many lives and that it continues to have its ripple effect. We who have benefitted from her wisdom and her friendship, her example and her faith – all of which manifested in the deep silent presence of the God who is love that pervaded her last days – it is we who will help her work and her vision continue to expand in this world of forms, just as she herself is expanding and dancing her way now in the world beyond form.

WORKS BY EILEEN O'HEA

Books

Silent Wisdom, Hidden Light, On Retreat With Series, Medio Media / Arthur James, UK, 1997. ISBN 9780853054252

Woman Her Intuition for Otherness: The Path of Christian Meditation, The Benedictine Priory, Montreal, Canada, 1989; Medio Media, USA,1990. ISBN 9780919815223

In Wisdom's Kitchen: The Process of Spiritual Direction, Continuum Publishing, New York and London, 2000. ISBN 9780826412355

Audio Recordings

Spirit and Psyche (Talks at John Main Seminar 1990), Medio Media, USA, 1991 (set of 5 audiotapes)

Silent Wisdom, Hidden Light: Christian Meditation and the Transformation of Consciousness, Medio Media, USA, 1995 (set of 2 audiotapes)

Rain for the Sea, Meditatio Talks Series, The World Community for Christian Meditation, Singapore, 2009

THE WORLD COMMUNITY FOR CHRISTIAN MEDITATION

www.wccm.org

John Main founded the first Christian Meditation Centre in London in 1975. The World Community for Christian Meditation (WCCM) took form in 1991 after the seed planted then had begun to grow into a far flung contemplative family. It now continues John Main's vision of restoring the contemplation dimension to the common life of the Church and to engage in dialogue in the common ground shared with the secular world and other religions.

The present director of the Community is Laurence Freeman, a student of John Main and a Benedictine monk of the Olivetan Congregation. The International Centre of the World Community is based in London with centres in many other parts of the world. The Community is a "monastery without walls", with both developed national organisation and emerging communities in over a hundred countries. A major building block of all this is the growing number of small, weekly meditation groups which meet in homes, parishes, offices, hospitals, prisons, and colleges. They form an ecumenical Christian community of diverse gifts and traditions.

Annually the John Main Seminar and the Way of Peace events bring meditators together in dialogue with other traditions and global movements. The Community also sponsors retreats, schools for the training of teachers of meditation, seminars, lectures, and other programmes. It contributes to interfaith dialogue particularly, in recent years, with Buddhists and Muslims. A quarterly spiritual letter with news of the Community is mailed and also available online. Weekly readings are available by email and a growing number of online resources are being developed to help the spiritual journey with the help of the latest technology. This enables new initiatives such as the teaching of meditation to children, networking young adult spirituality and the contemplative dimension of the life of priests. Medio Media is the publishing arm of the community producing a wide range of books and audio-visual titles to support the practice of meditation.

MEDITATIO is the outreach of the World Community initiated to mark its twentieth anniversary. Coordinated from the MEDITATIO Centre in London, a programme of seminars will bring a spiritual approach to key social issues of our time such as education, mental health, peace and justice, business, care for those in recovery and the dying. MEDITATIO is developing the use of technology in the work of spiritual renewal. It will also help with the formation of a younger generation of meditators who will serve later as leaders of the community.

THE WORLD COMMUNITY FOR CHRISTIAN MEDITATION
www.wccm.org

WCCM Centres and Contacts Worldwide

For more information about the Community, its work and publications, to join a meditation group, or to learn to meditate, please contact your regional coordinator below or the International Centre.

INTERNATIONAL CENTRE

The World Community for Christian Meditation
St Mark's, Myddelton Square
London EC1R 1XX, UK
Tel +44 20 7278 2070
Fax +44 20 7713 6346
welcome@wccm.org
www.wccm.org

FOR COUNTRIES NOT LISTED BELOW,
CONTACT THE INTERNATIONAL CENTRE.

Argentina www.meditacioncristianagrupos.blogspot.com
Australia www.christianmeditationaustralia.org
Barbados pookshill@caribsurf.com

Belgium www.christmed.be

Brazil www.wccm.com.br

Canada English www.meditatio.ca

Canada French www.meditationchretienne.ca

Chile www.meditacioncristiana.cl

China www.wccm.hk

Colombia www.meditacioncristianacol.blogspot.com

Curacao cratz@cura.net

Czech Republic www.krestanskameditace.cz

Denmark www.kristenmeditation.org

Ecuador raul.guzman@cablemodem.com.ec

Fiji frdenis@connect.com.fj

Finland timo.huotari@ymail.com

France www.meditationchretienne.org

Germany www.wccm.de

Haiti inobert@yahoo.fr

Hong Kong www.wccm.hk

India www.wccm-india.org/

Indonesia www.meditasikristiani.com

Ireland www.christianmeditation.ie

Italy www.meditazionecristiana.org

Japan www.esuk.net/wccm

Latvia www.jesus.lv

Lithuania rkorvel@almi-decor.com

Malaysia wccm.malaysia@gmail.com

Malta www.wccmalta.org

Mauritius miriamboyle@yahoo.com

Mexico www.meditacioncristiana.com

Netherlands www.wccm.nl

New Zealand www.christianmeditationnz.org.nz

Nicaragua jorgefnsc@yahoo.com

Northern Ireland - Belfast philomenamcquillan1@hotmail.co.uk

Norway www.wccm.no

Pakistan amirjacob@yahoo.com

Papua New Guinea Sr Francisca Petros, PO Box 69 Mendi PNG

Paraguay adacenturion@gmail.com

Peru titojulis@gmail.com

Philippines czgomez123@yahoo.com

Poland www.wccm.pl

Portugal www.meditacaocrista.com

Russia www.wccm.org.ua

Singapore www.wccmsingapore.org

Solomon Islands paroi@solomon.com.sb

South Africa www.wccm.co.za

Spain Catalonia www.meditaciocristiana.cat/

Spain en Espanol www.meditacioncristiana.com/

Sri Lanka silvaimmaculata@yahoo.com

Switzerland deborah.walton@gmai.com

Tahiti Elivre.cholet@mail.pf

Tanzania njeretherese@yahoo.com

Thailand bkkemilie@gmail.com

Trinidad – West Indies ruthsjc@flowtrinidad.net

Uganda robert.seruwagi@barclays.com

Ukraine http://wccm.org.ua

United Kingdom www.christian-meditation.org.uk

United States www.wccm-usa.org

Uruguay decker26@gmail.com

Venezuela http://meditadores.blogspot.com

Vietnam tinvuicfc@gmail.com

Zambia pierpaolomonella@googlemail.co